Whitby Ontario Book 1 in Colour Photos, Saving Our History One Photo at a Time

Photography
by Barbara Raué
2022

Series Name: Cruising Ontario

Book 201: Whitby Book 1

Cover photo: 213 Byron Street South/101 Dunlop Street West, Page 35

Series Name: Cruising Ontario
Saving Our History One Photo at a Time
in colour photos

Books Available in Alphabetical Order:
Aberfoyle, Acton, Alton, Amherstburg, Ancaster, Arthur, Auburn, Aylmer, Ayr, Beaver Valley, Belgrave, Belleville, Bloomingdale, Blyth, Brantford, Brockville, Burford, Burlington, Caledon, Caledonia, Cambridge, Carlow, Chatsworth, Clifford, Collingwood, Conestogo, Delhi, Dorchester to Aylmer, Drayton, Drumbo, Dundas, Dunlop, Eden Mills, Elmira, Elora, Erin, Essex, Fergus, Goderich, Grimsby, Guelph, Hagersville, Hamilton, Hanover, Harriston, Hespeler, Jarvis, Kingston, Kingsville, Kitchener, Lake Superior, Lincoln, Linwood, Listowel, London, Lucknow, Merrickville, Mono, Mount Forest, Mount Pleasant, Neustadt, New Hamburg, Newboro, Newport, Niagara-on-the-Lake, Oakville, Onondaga, Orangeville, Orillia, Owen Sound, Palmerston, Paris, Pelham, Perth, Peterborough, Petrolia, Port Colborne, Port Elgin, Portland, Preston, Rockwood, Sarnia, Sault Ste. Marie, Seaforth, Sheffield, Shelburne, Simcoe, Smiths Falls, Smithville, Southampton, St. Catharines, St. George, St. Jacobs, St. Marys, St. Thomas, Stoney Creek, Stratford, Thamesford, Thunder Bay, Tillsonburg, Toronto, Waterdown, Waterford, Waterloo, Welland, Wellesley, West Flamborough, Westport, Whitby, Windsor, Wingham, Woodstock

Book 198: Chatsworth
Book 199: Wingham
Book 200: West Flamborough
Book 201-202: Whitby

Table of Contents

Centre Street	Page 6
King Street	Page 22
St. John Street West	Page 27
Colborne Street West	Page 32
Byron Street South	Page 33
Dunlop Street West	Page 51
Walnut Street	Page 52
Mary Street West	Page 55
Brock Street South	Page 56
Brock Street North	Page 64

Whitby is located in Durham Region in Southern Ontario, east of Ajax and west of Oshawa, on the north shore of Lake Ontario. It is about twenty kilometers (twelve miles) east of the Toronto borough of Scarborough. The southern part of Whitby is predominantly urban and an economic hub; the northern part is more rural and includes the communities of Ashburn, Brooklin, Myrtle, and Myrtle Station.

Whitby was named after the seaport town of Whitby, Yorkshire, England. Settlement dates back to 1800, however, it was not until 1836 that a downtown business center was established by Whitby's founder Peter Perry. Whitby's chief asset was its natural harbor on Lake Ontario, from which grain from the farmland to the north was first shipped in 1833. In the 1840s, a road was built from Whitby Harbor to Lake Simcoe and Georgian Bay, to bring trade and settlement through the harbor to and from the rich land to the north.

Many residents commute to work in other Greater Toronto Area communities, and General Motors Canada in Oshawa is a major employer for all of Durham Region. Whitby has a steel mill, a retail support center operated by Sobeys, and a major Liquor Control Board of Ontario warehouse.

Four railways pass through Whitby. The Toronto-Montreal corridor main lines of the Canadian National Railway and Canadian Pacific Railway both pass east–west through the south end of town. A second CP line running from Toronto to Havelock passes through the northern part of Whitby. Via Rail trains travel through Whitby, but the nearest station is in Oshawa. GO Transit provides frequent service via its Lakeshore East line.

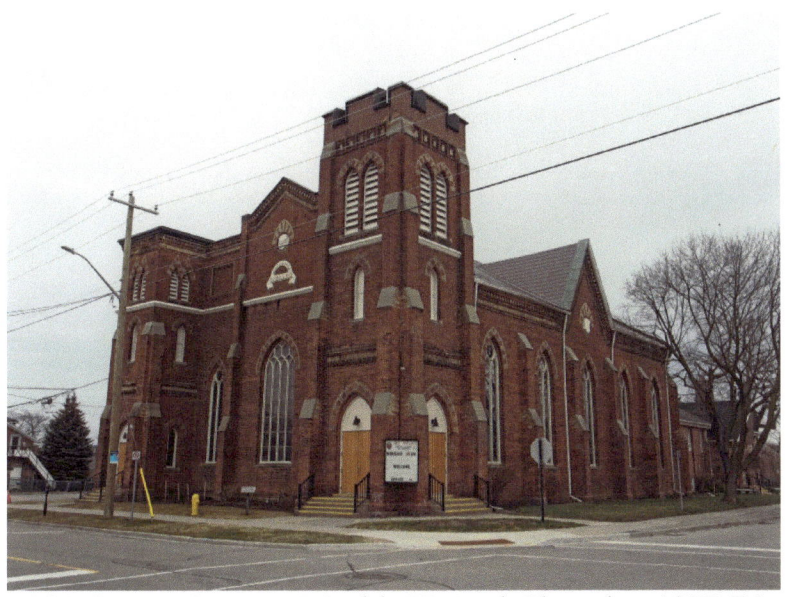

201 Centre Street – Mark's United Church – 1875-76

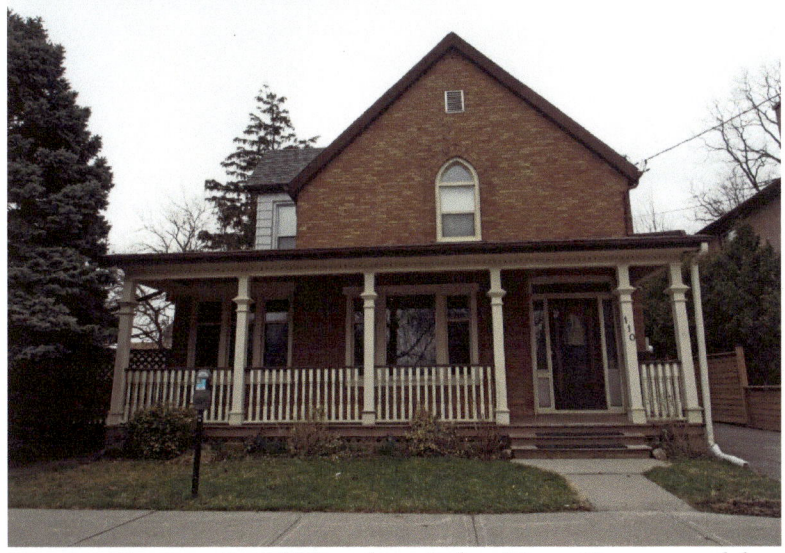

110 Centre Street – In 1877, when John Ham Perry could no longer afford to maintain his 'castle' (which stood on what is now Kinsmen Park), he moved to this house and lived here for nineteen years until his death.

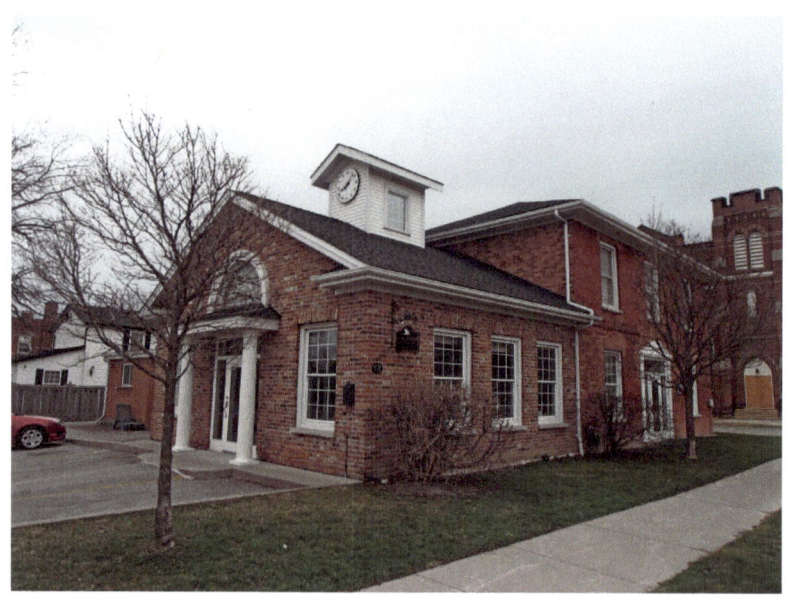

109 Centre Street South/218 Colborne Street West – Alexander McPherson House - 1852

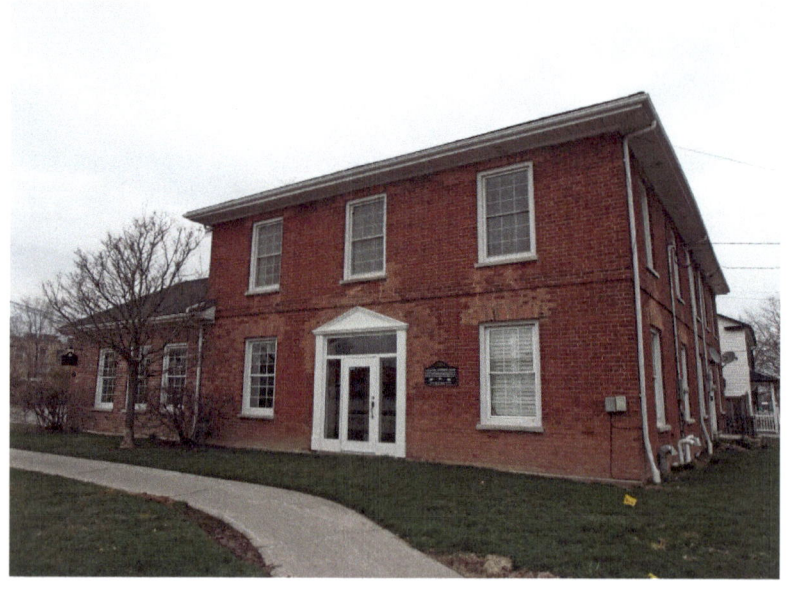

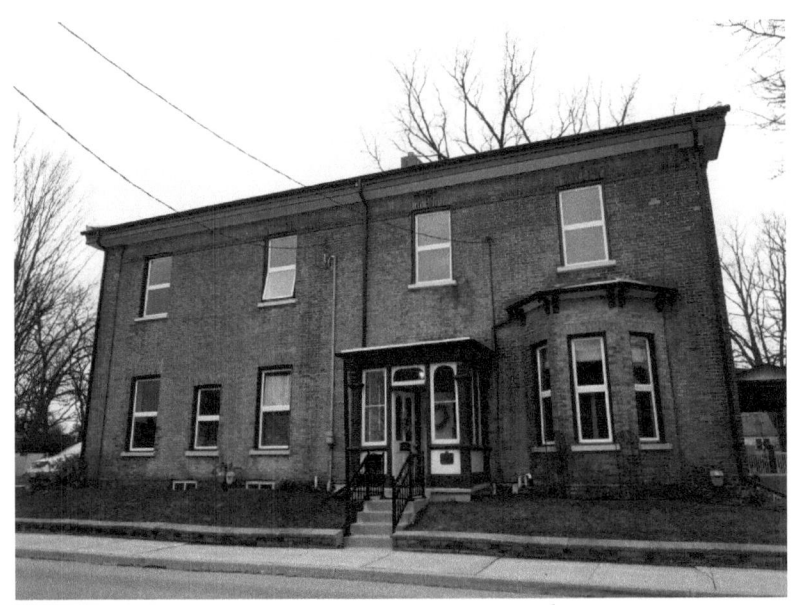

202 Centre Street South

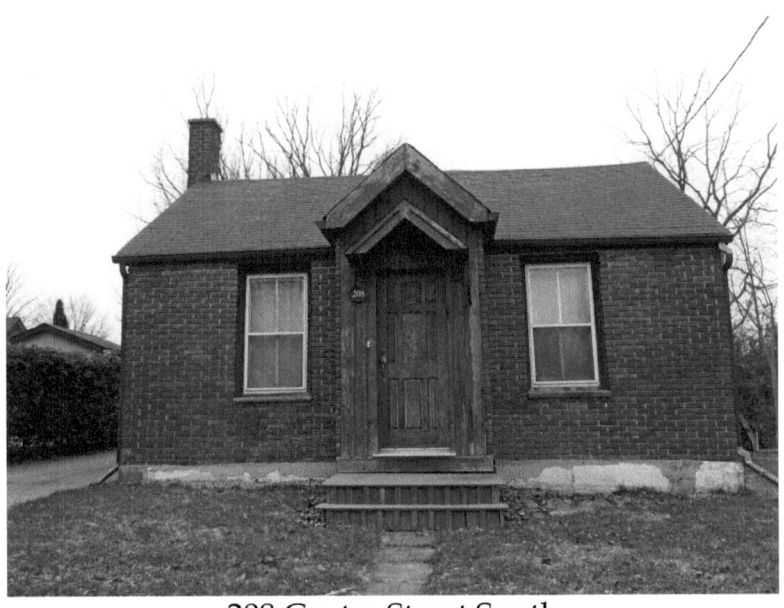

208 Centre Street South

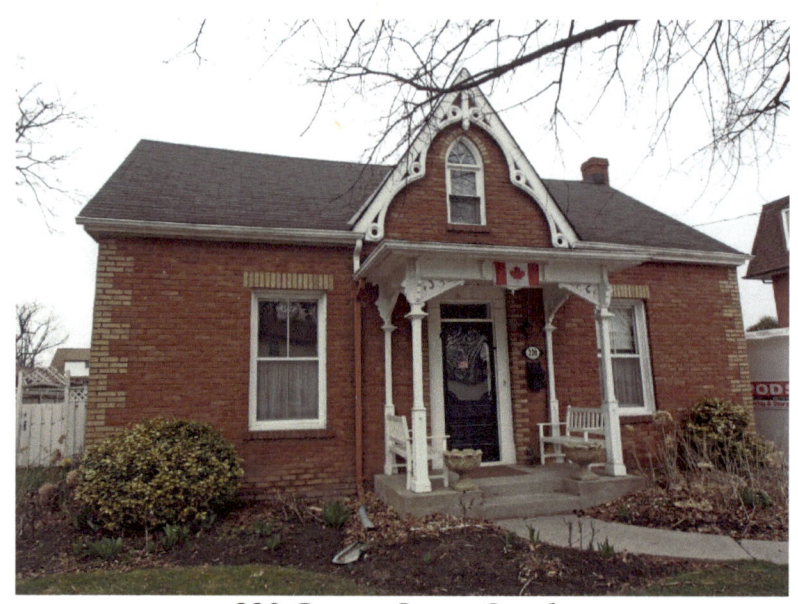

220 Centre Street South

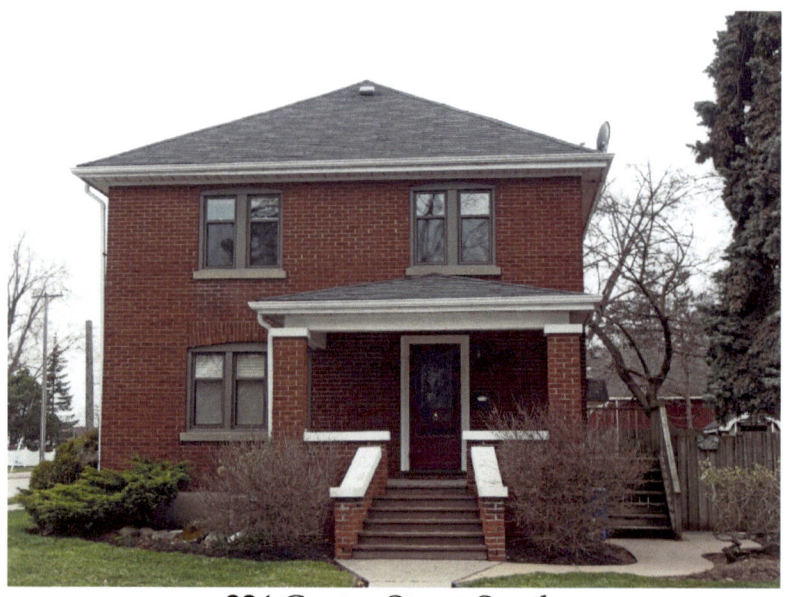

224 Centre Street South

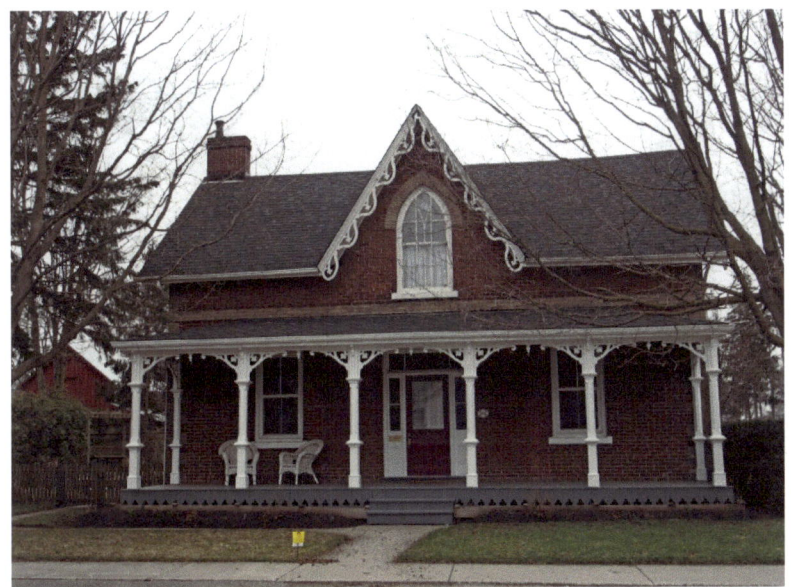

300 Centre Street South – Holden Jackson House - 1869

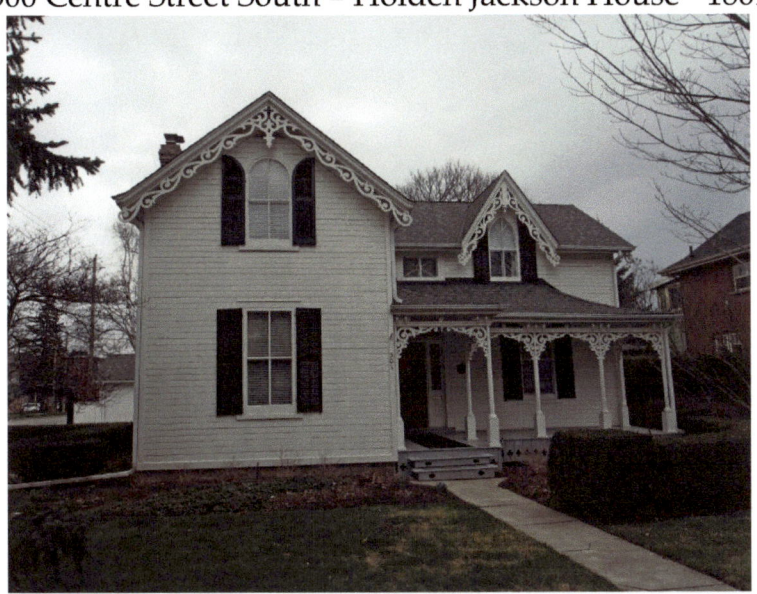

301 Centre Street South – c. 1875 – built for William Hood, a retired Whitby farmer and son of an English settler – rubble-stone foundation, white clapboard building, two-story vernacular Gothic Revival

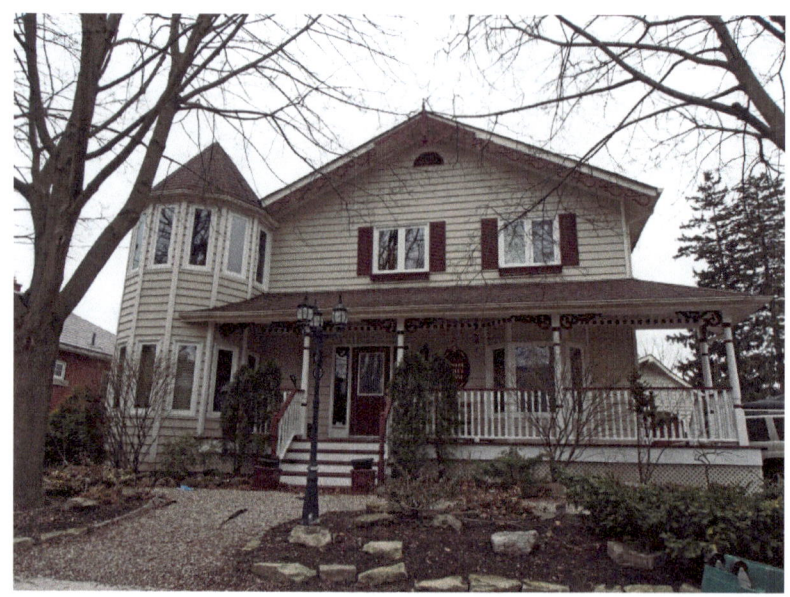

302 Centre Street South

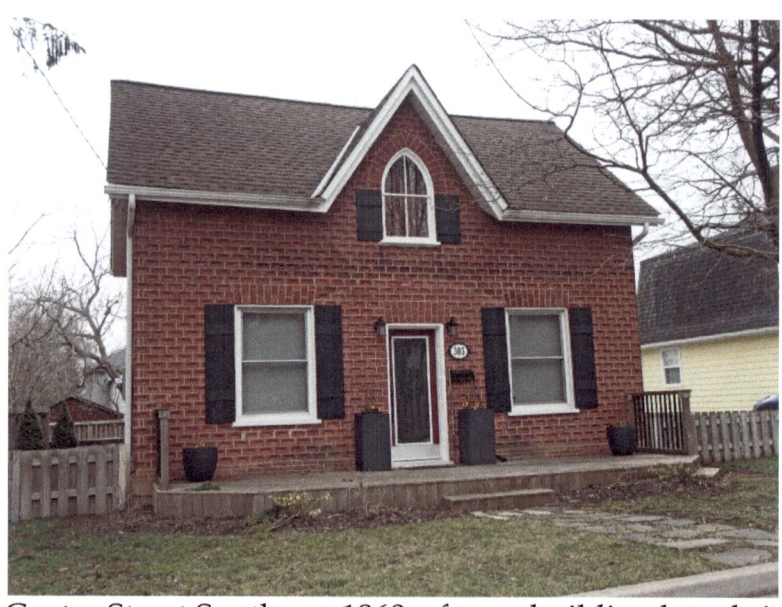

305 Centre Street South – c. 1860 – frame building later bricked over

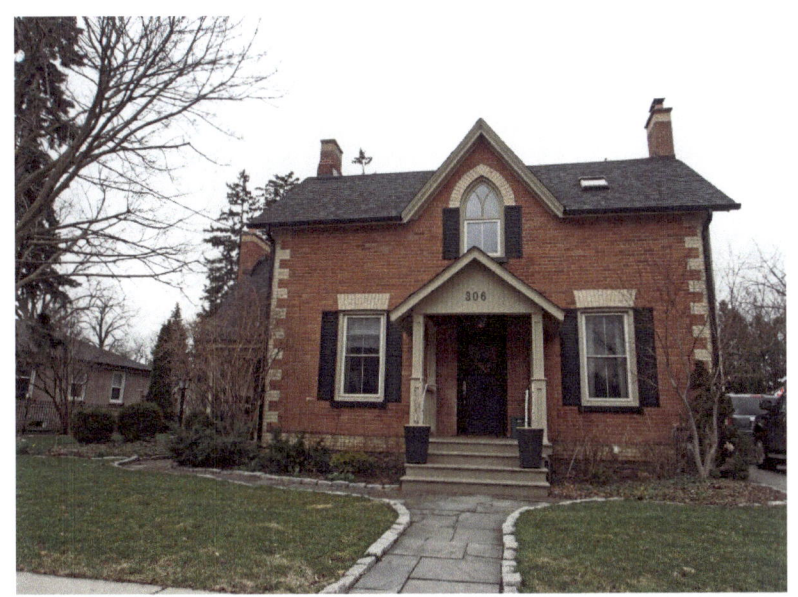

306 Centre Street South – c. 1875 – Victorian Gothic style

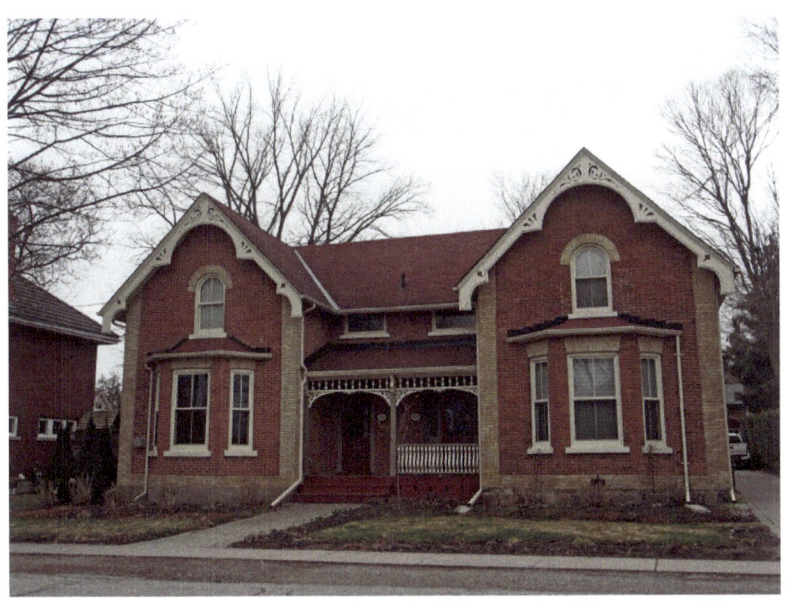

308-310 Centre Street South – William A. Hannam House - 1877

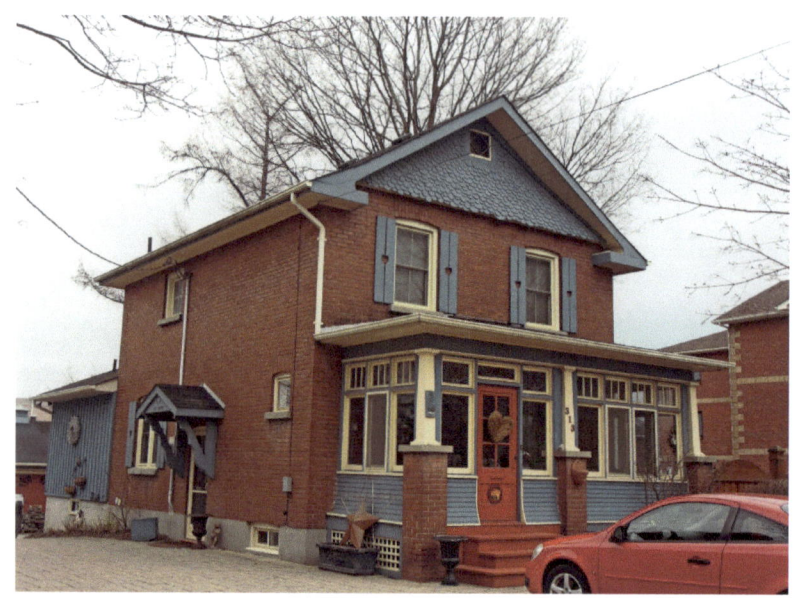

313 Centre Street South

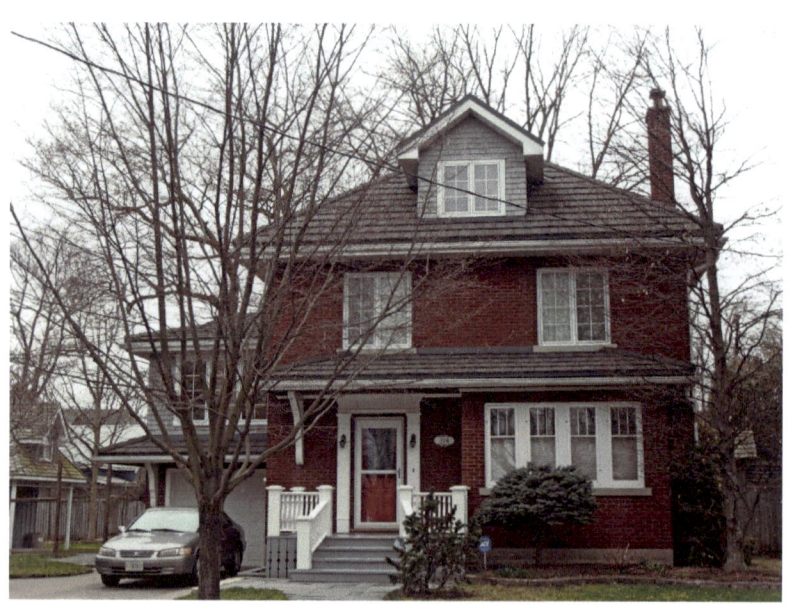

314 Centre Street South

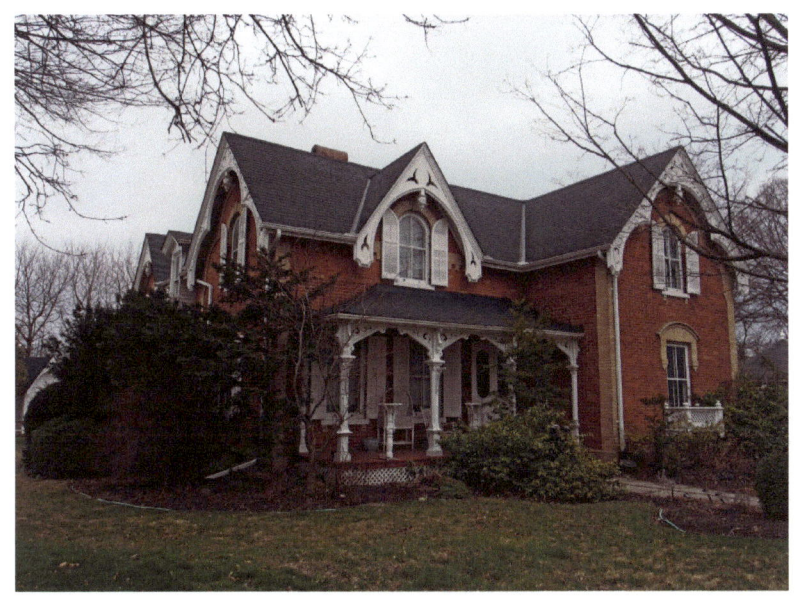

Centre Street South

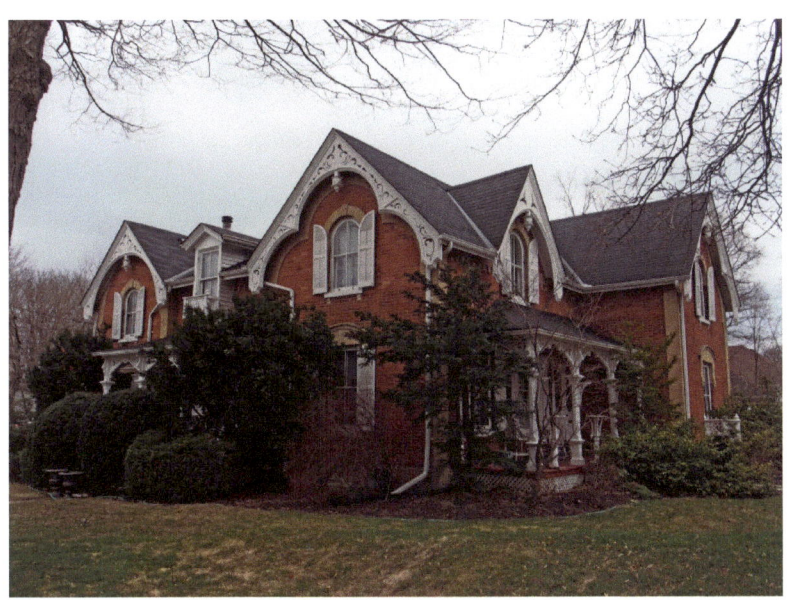

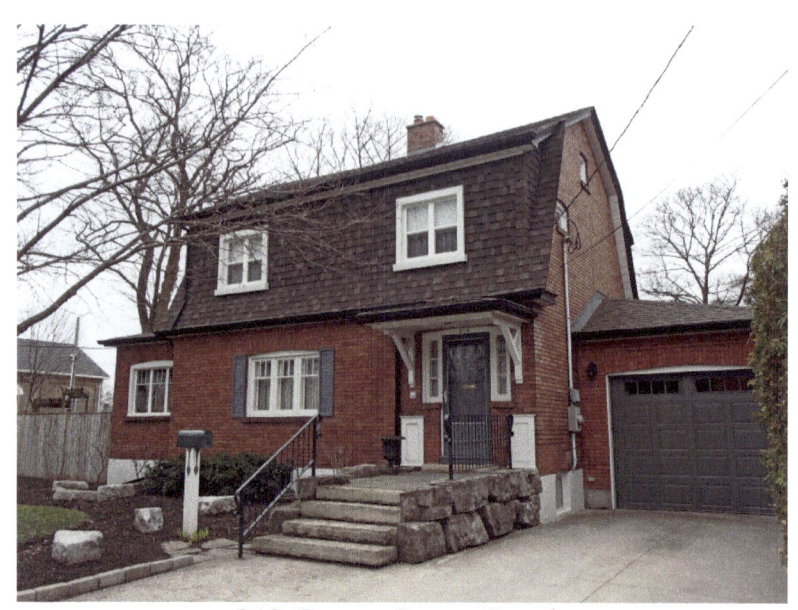

313 Centre Street South

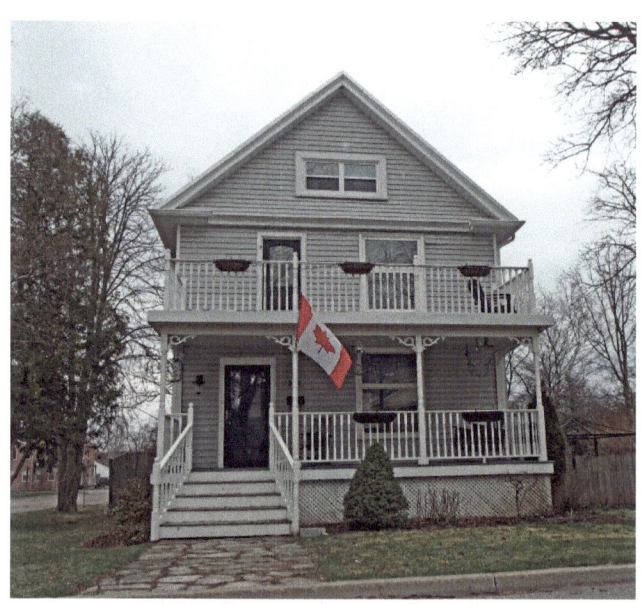

331 Centre Street South

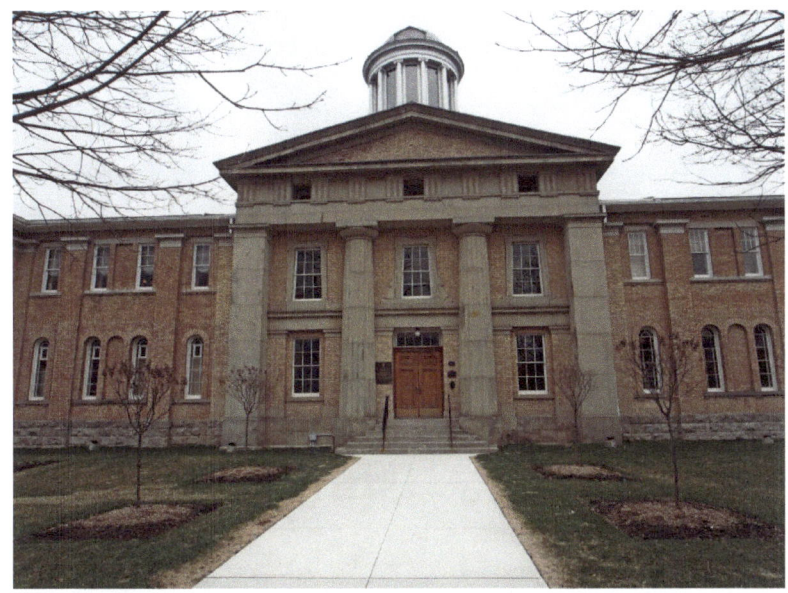

416 Centre Street South – Whitby Centennial Building was designed by Cumberland and Strom in the Greek Revival style. It was built in 1853 with the second floor added in 1910. It served as Ontario County Court House from 1854 to 1964.

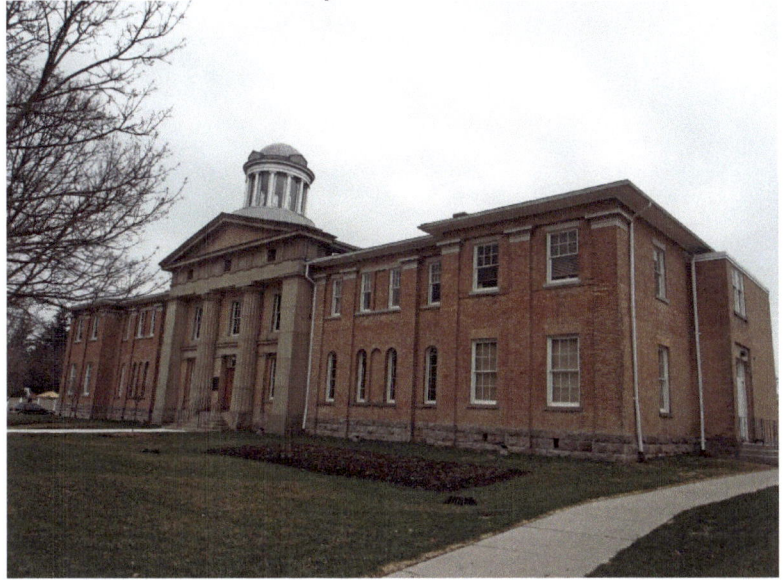

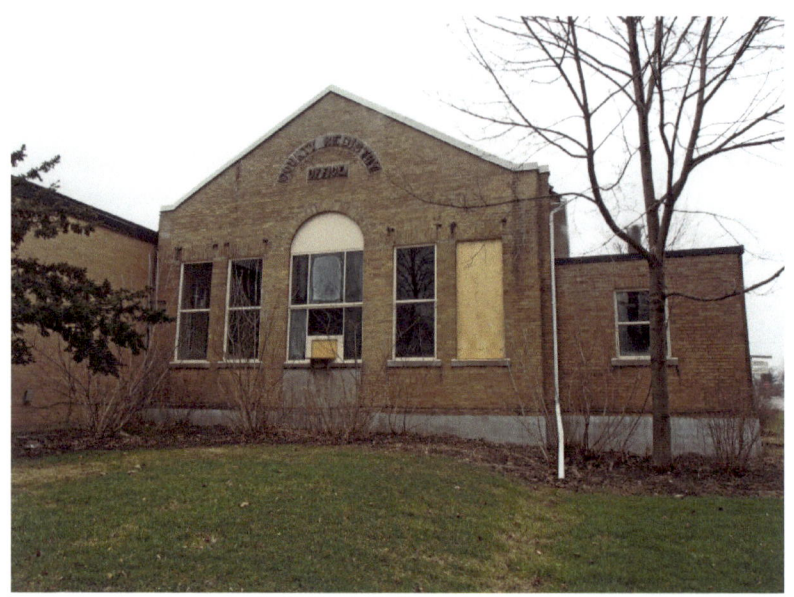

400 Centre Street South – County Registry Office - 1873

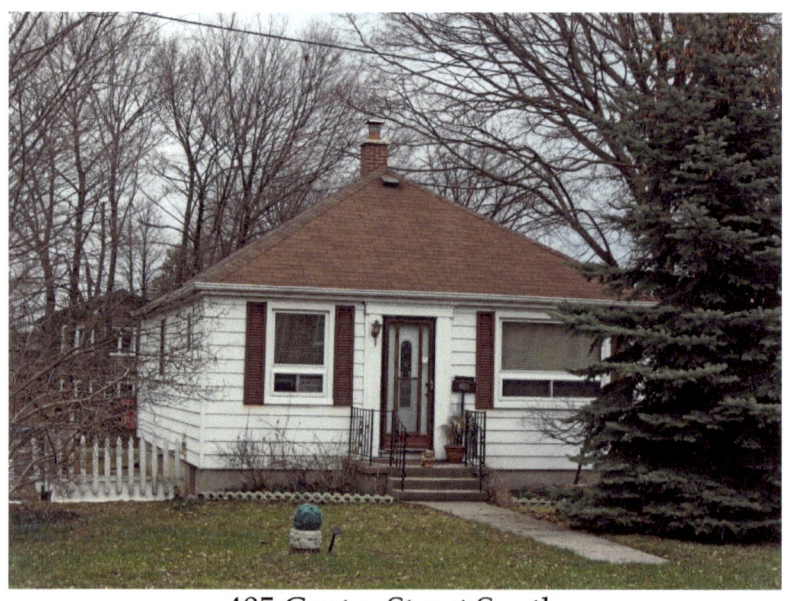

405 Centre Street South

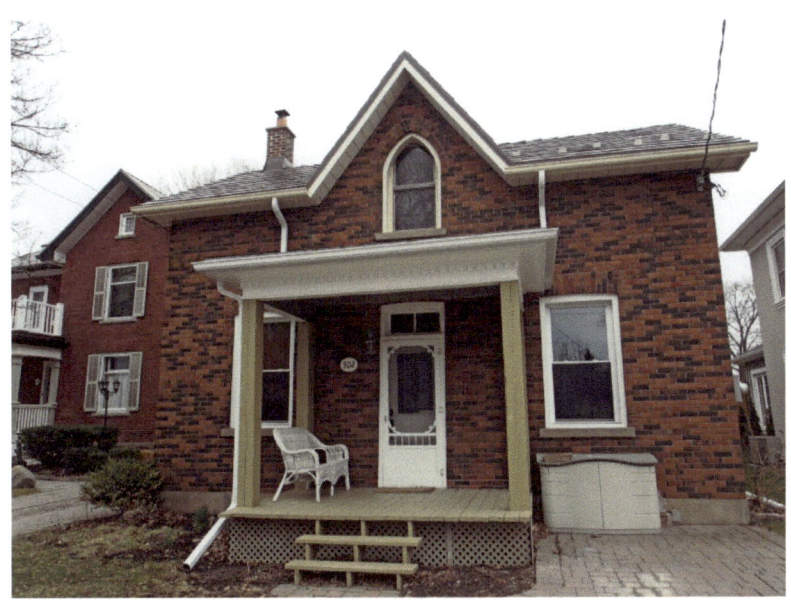

502 Centre Street South - 1854

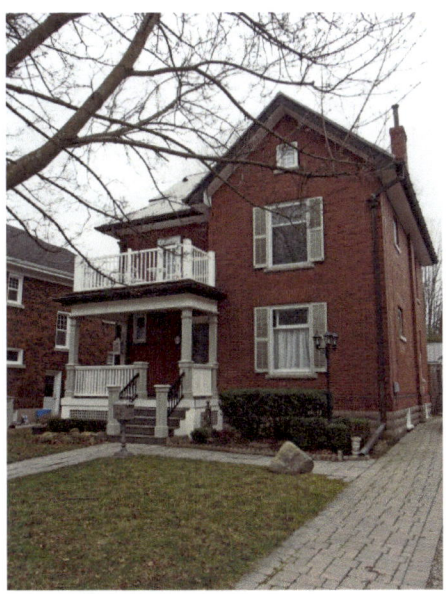

504 Centre Street South

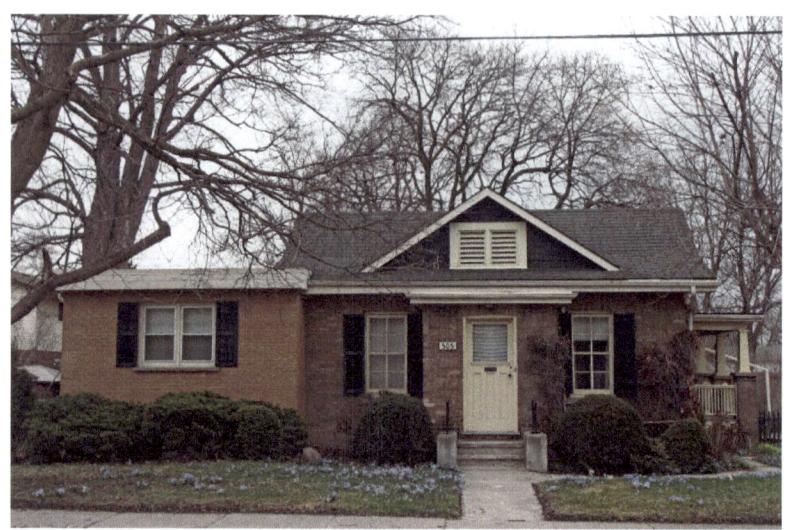
505 Centre Street South - 1930

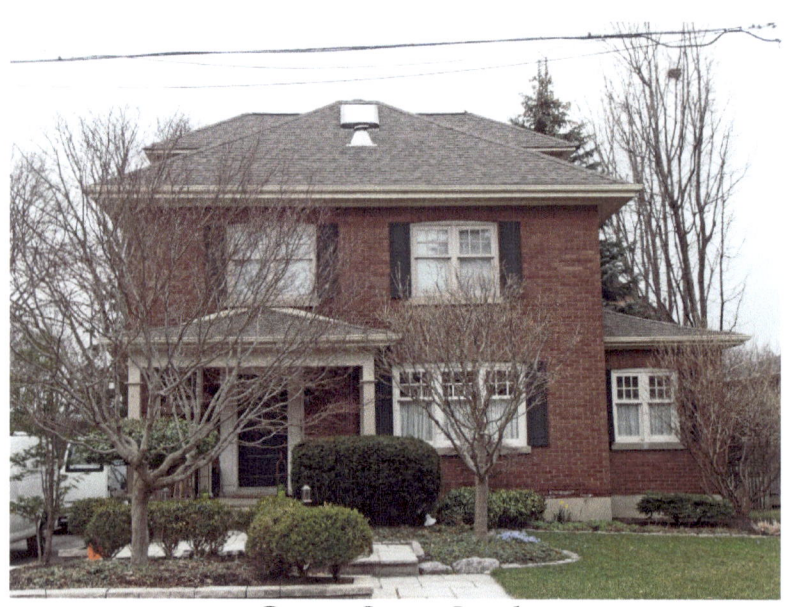
Centre Street South

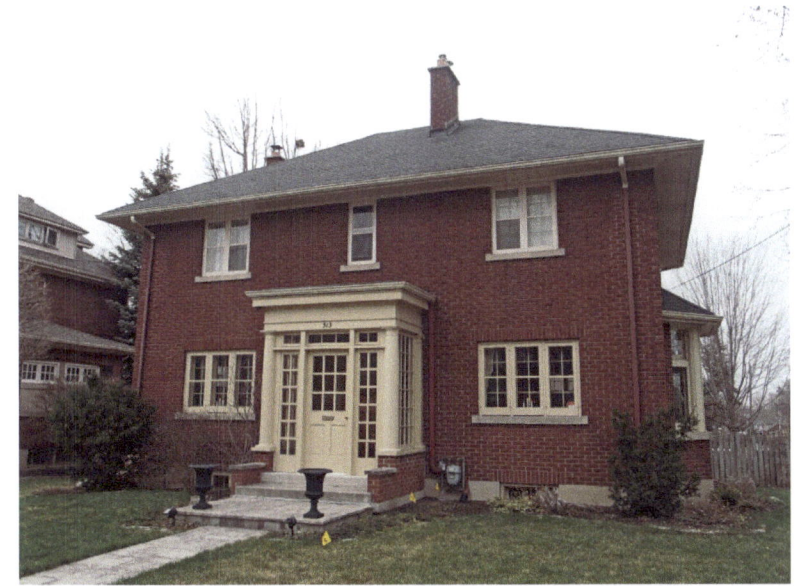

513 Centre Street South – Arthur Archibald House - 1928

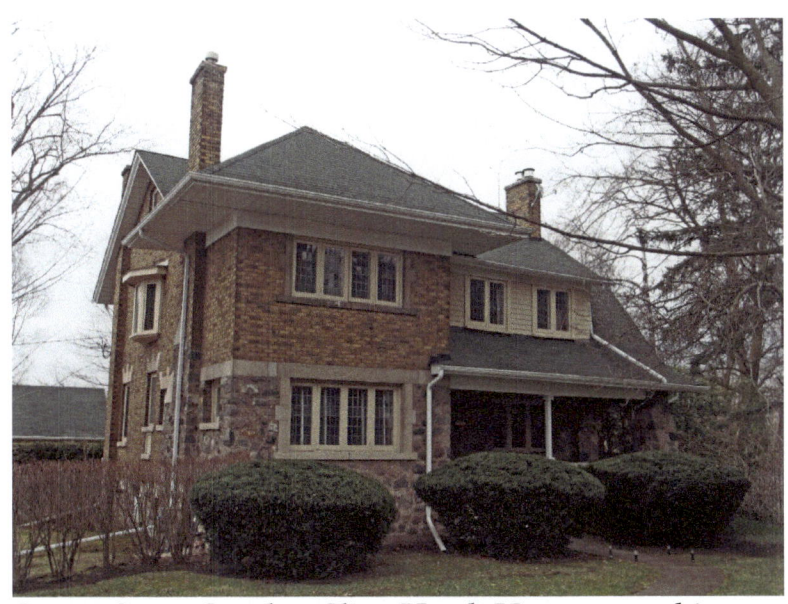

601 Centre Street South – Clive Hatch House - combines elements of the Prairie style architecture and Arts & Crafts style – c. 1915

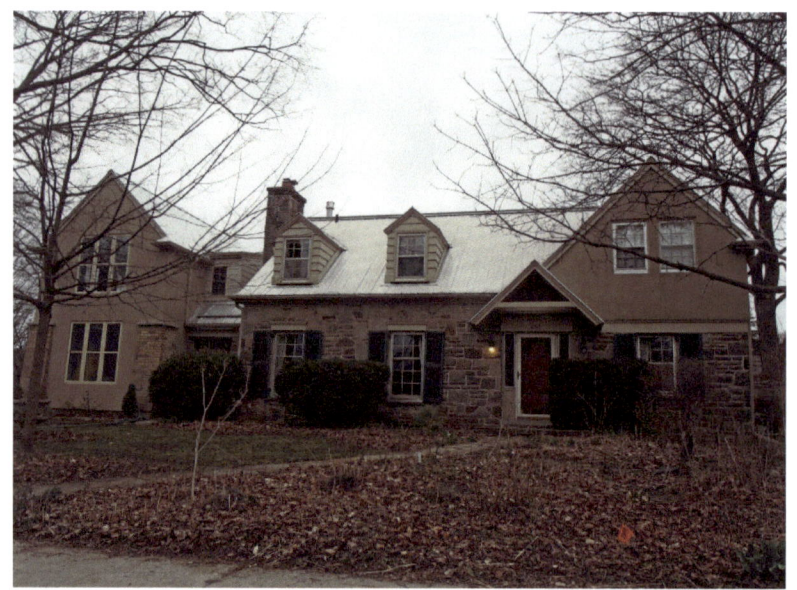

696 Centre Street South

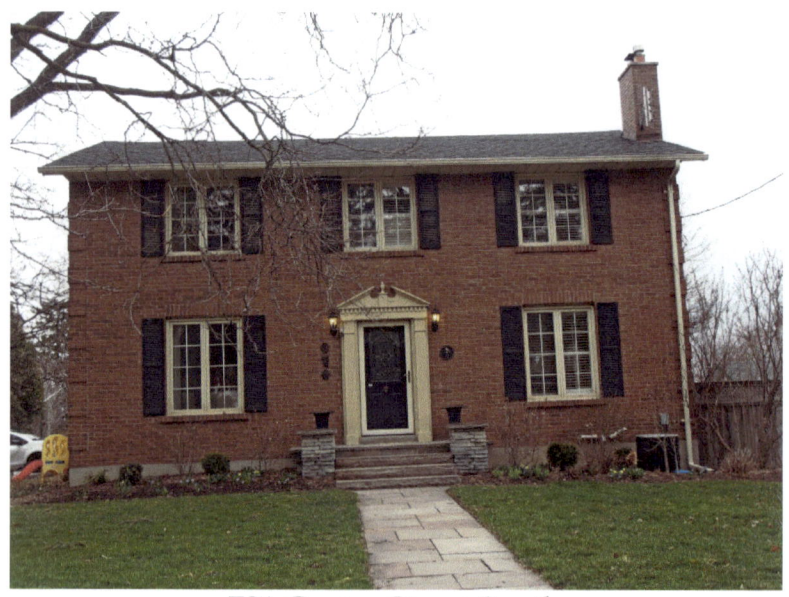

701 Centre Street South

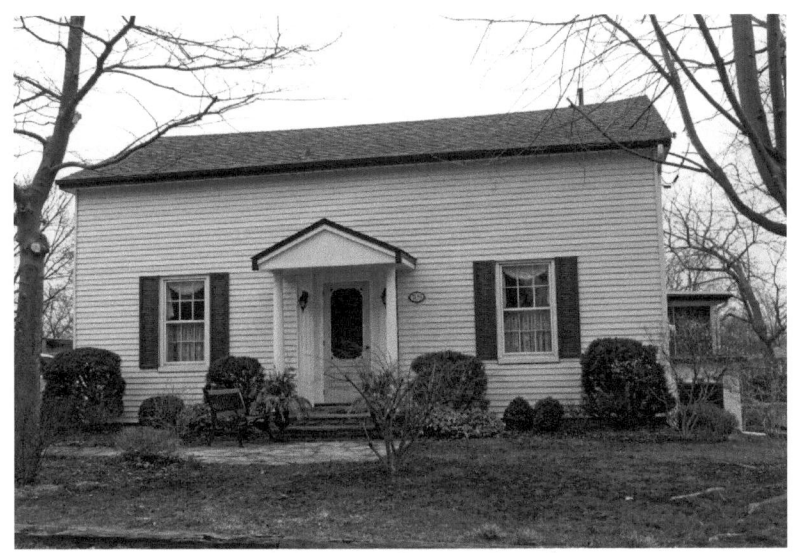

709 Centre Street South

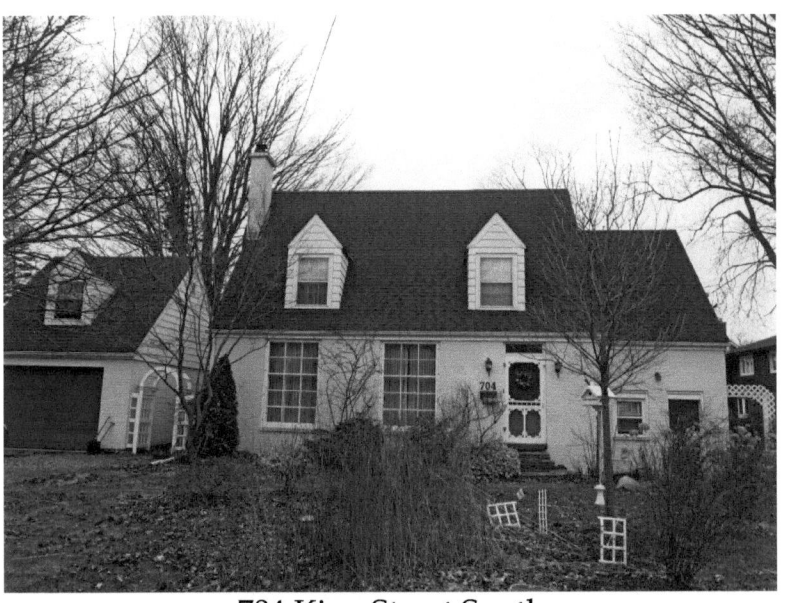

704 King Street South

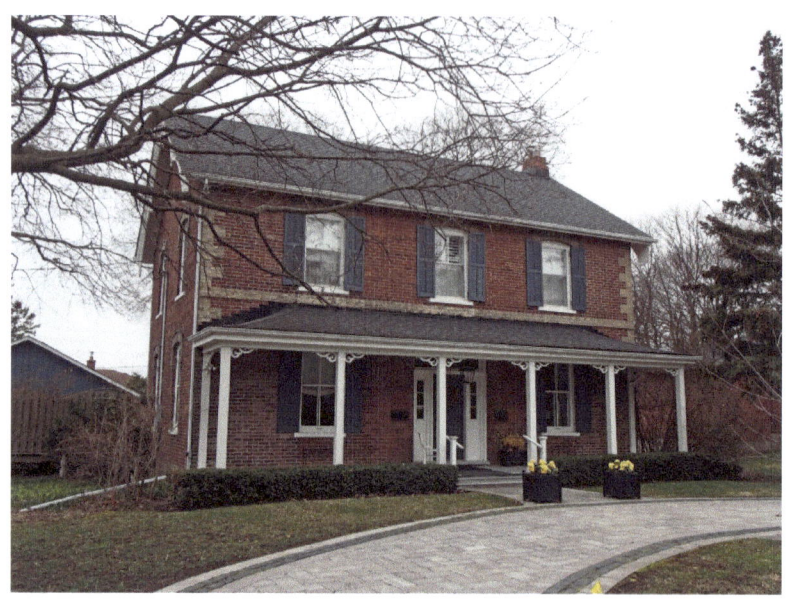

616 King Street – c. 1776 – Green-Lawlor House - Neo-Classical with Gothic Revival details of the bargeboards

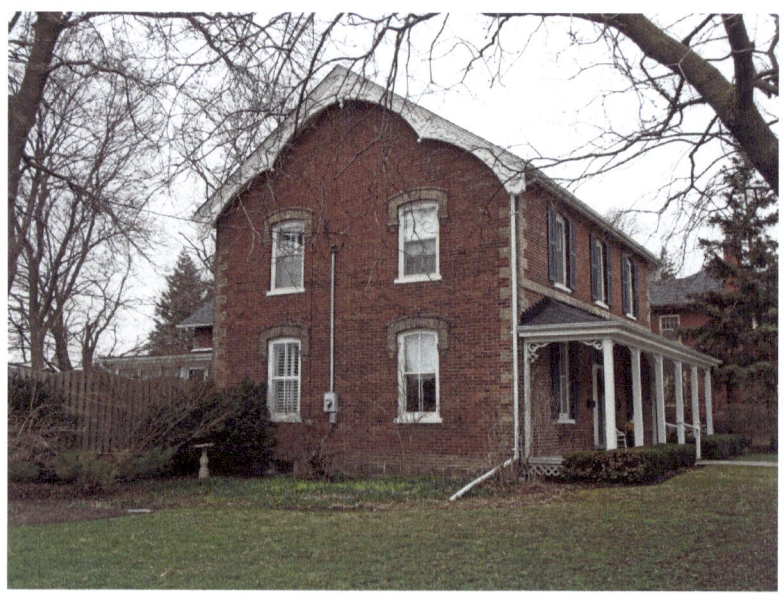

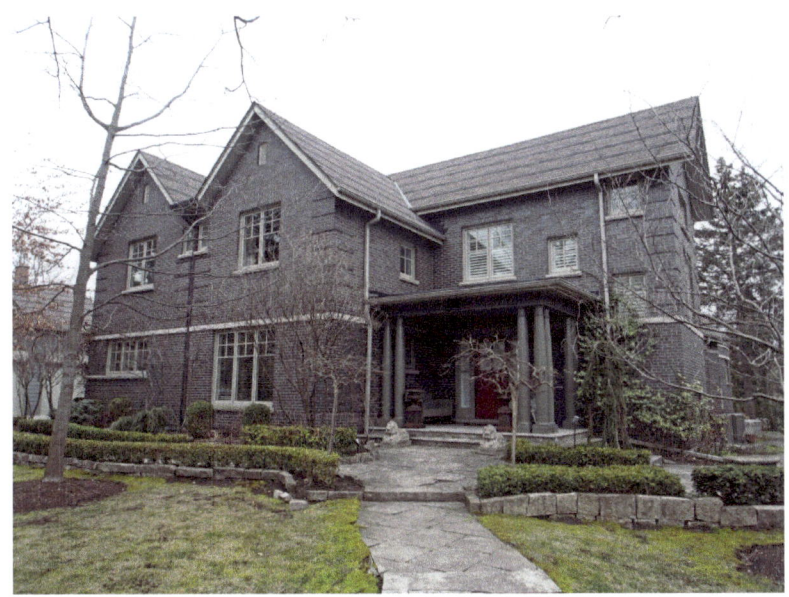

611 King Street

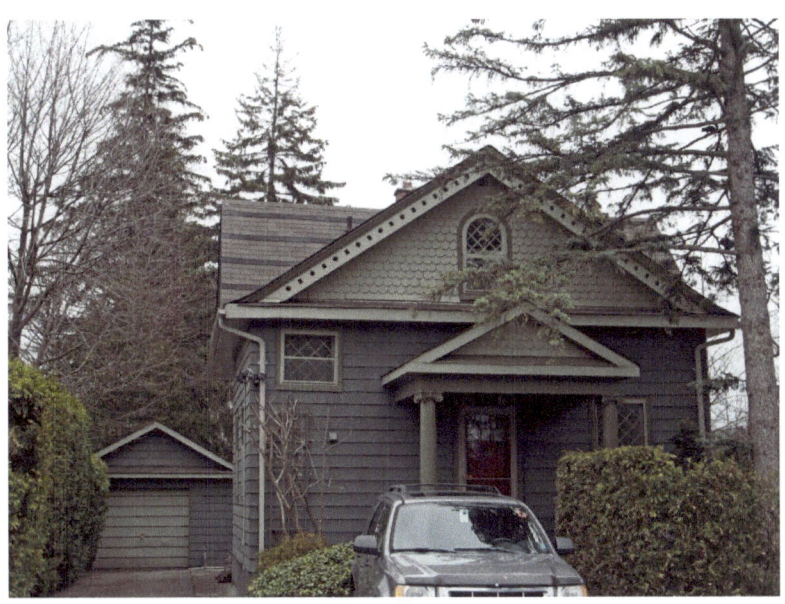

King Street

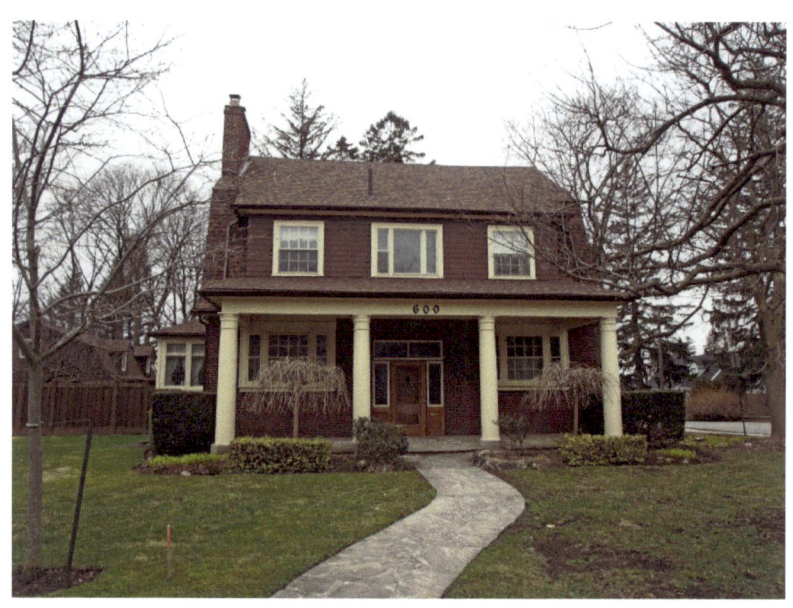

600 King Street – c. 1913 – gambrel roof – built for Dr. Horace Bascom who was Clerk of the Ontario County Court from 1912-55

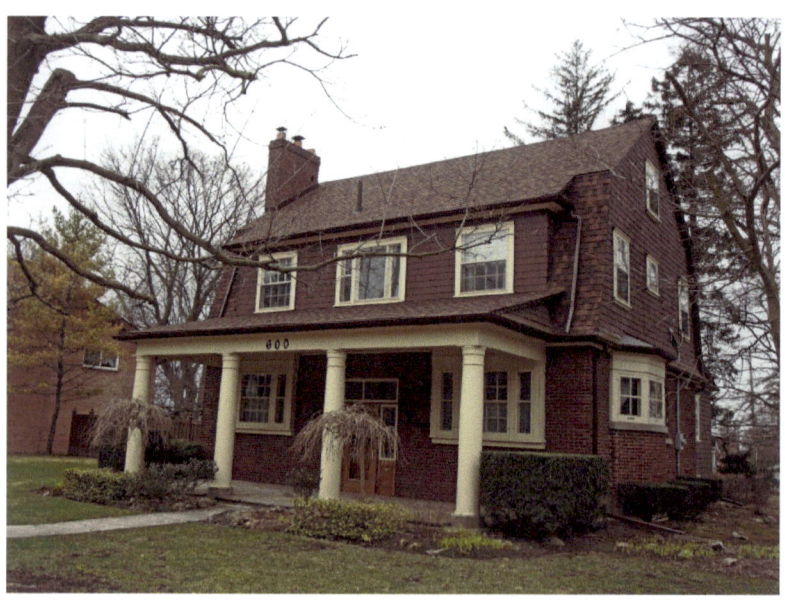

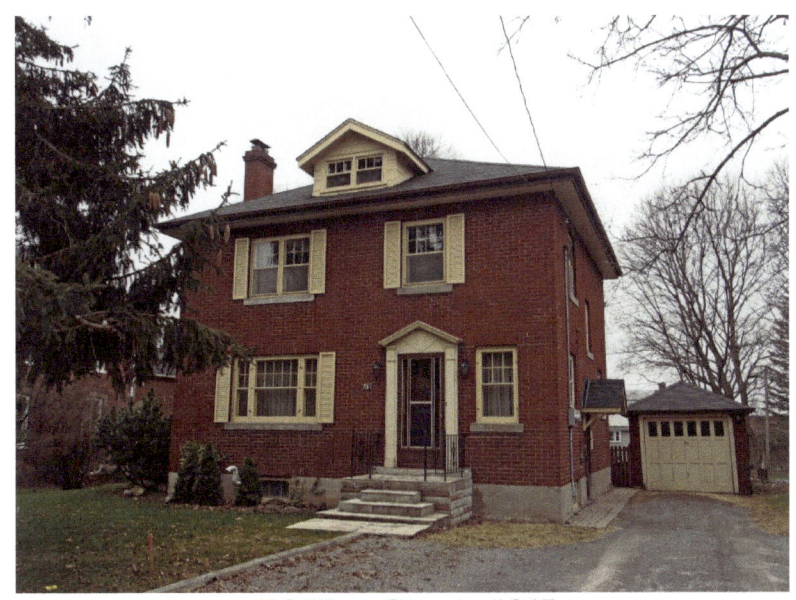

610 King Street - 1945

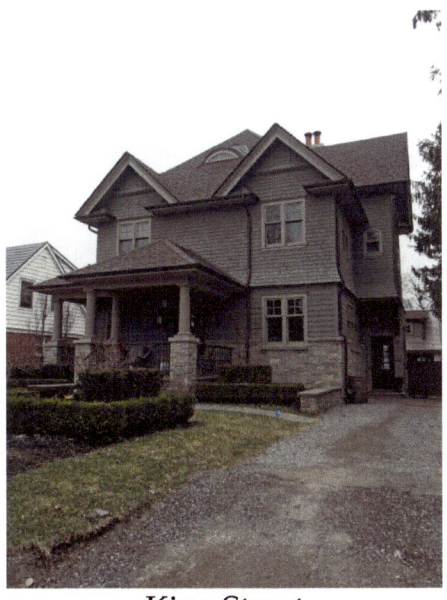

King Street

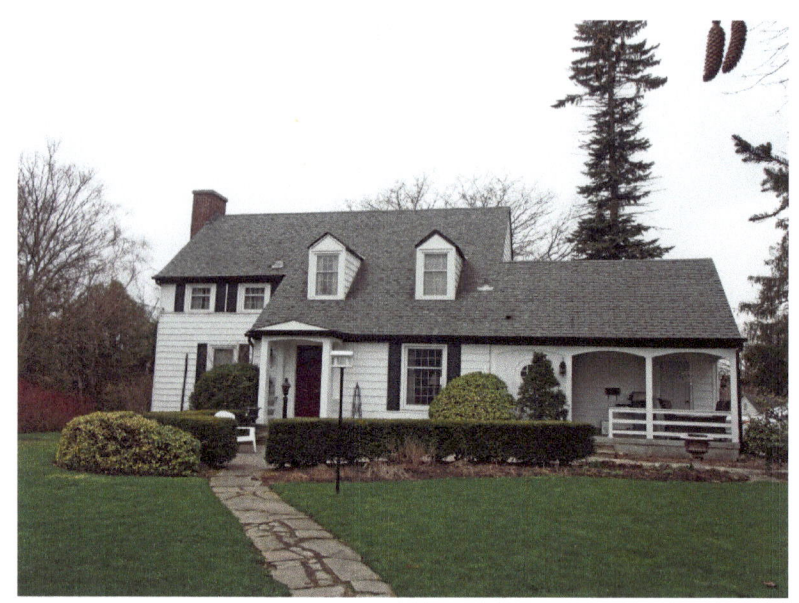

500 King Street - 1941

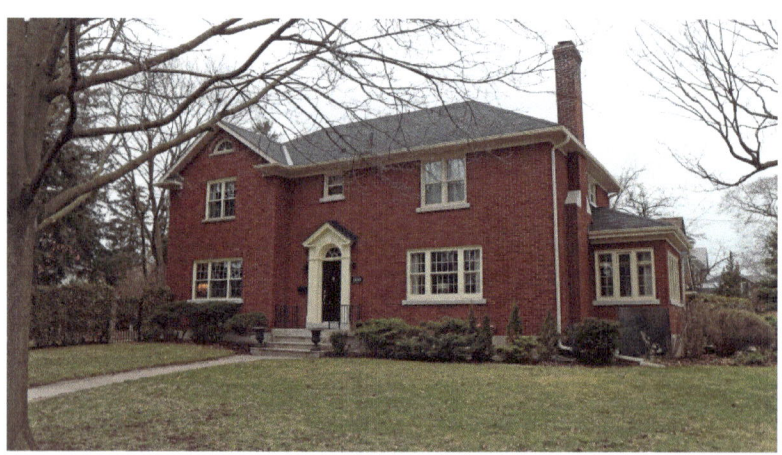

300 St. John Street West

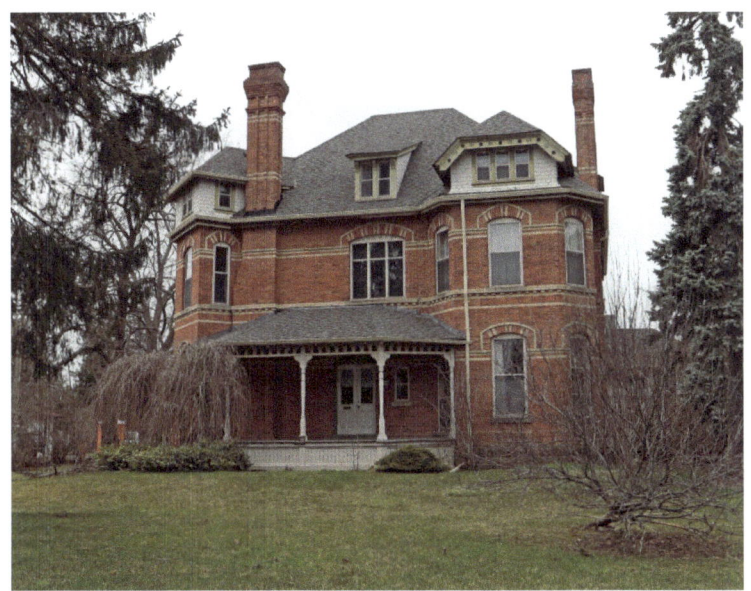

320 St. John Street West – c. 1881 – designed by Canadian architect, Henry Langley – high Victorian style – built for Judge George Dartnell – From 1899 to 1920, it was the home of Judge Duncan John McIntyre.

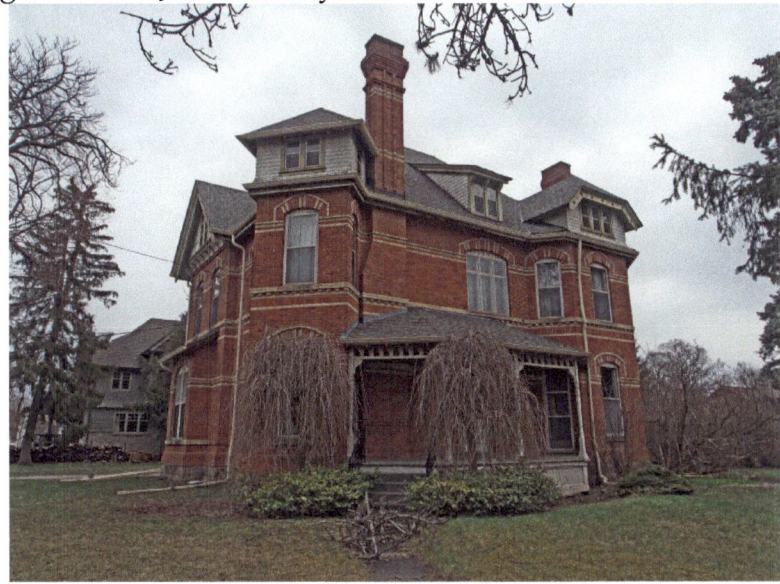

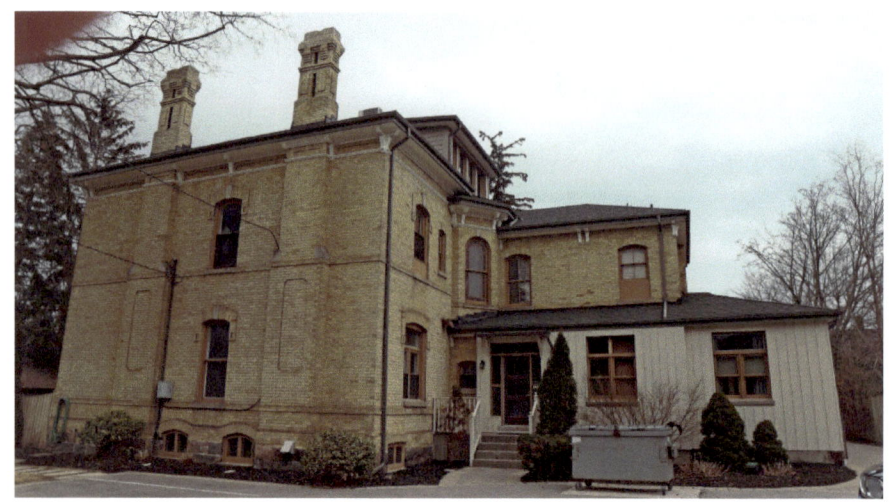
St. John Street West

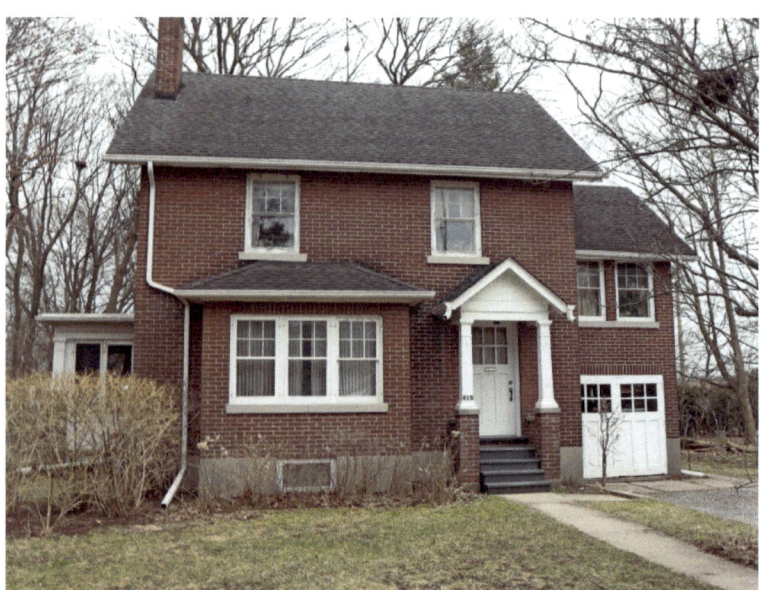
415 St. John Street West – 1931 – Rev. Arthur Mansell Irwin House

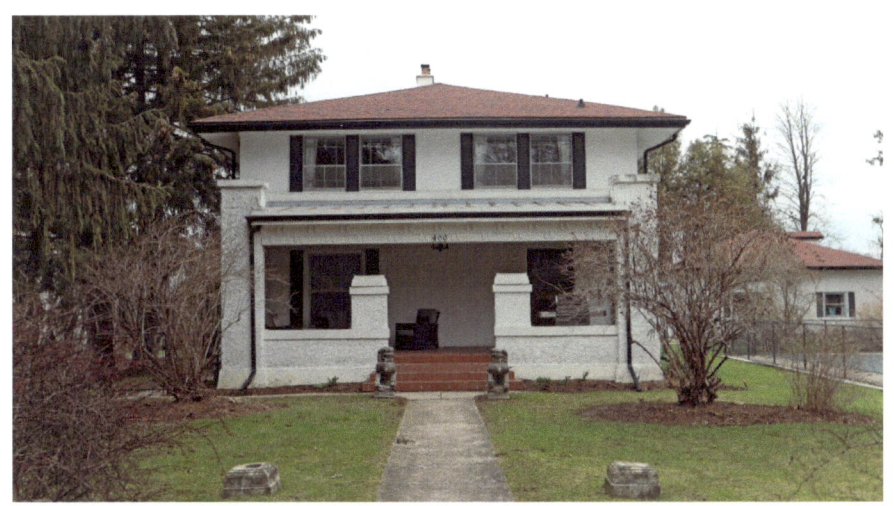

400 St. John Street West – c. 1913 – Prairie style – built for George Dryden, Registrar of Deeds for Ontario County from 1897 to 1931

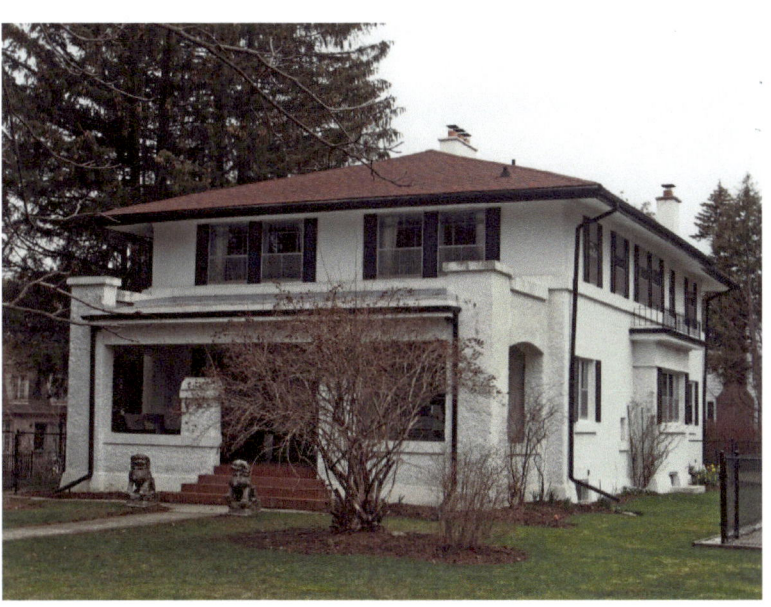

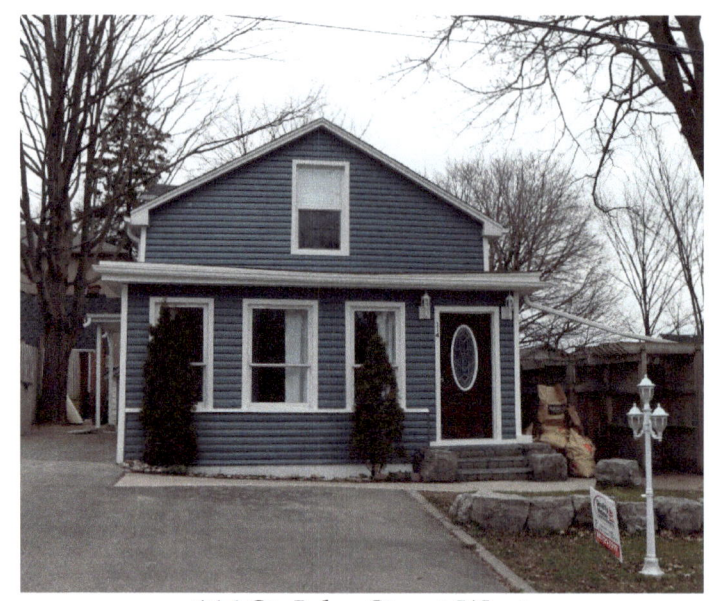

114 St. John Street West

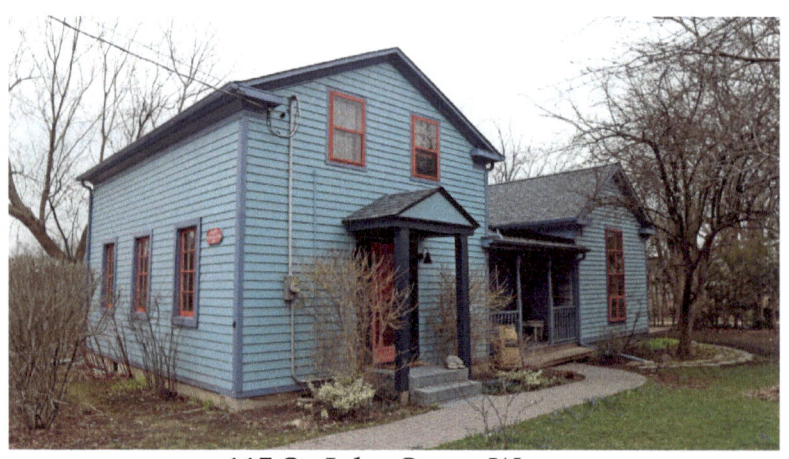

115 St. John Street West

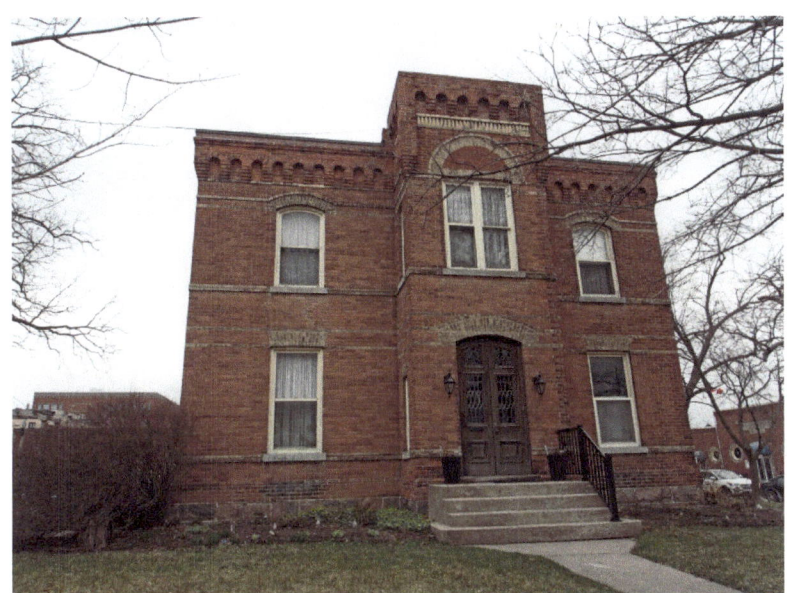

200 Colborne Street West - George Conrad Gross House –
Castle Style house built in Gothic Revival style - c. 1883

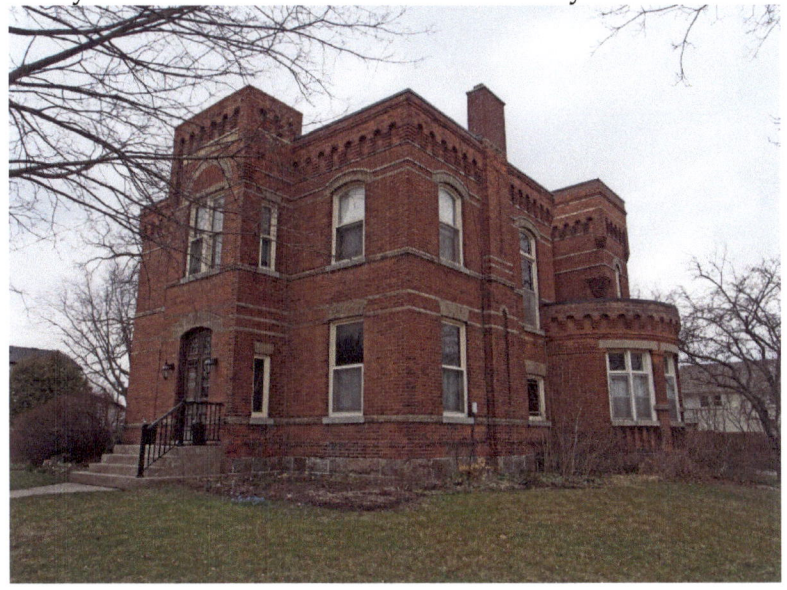

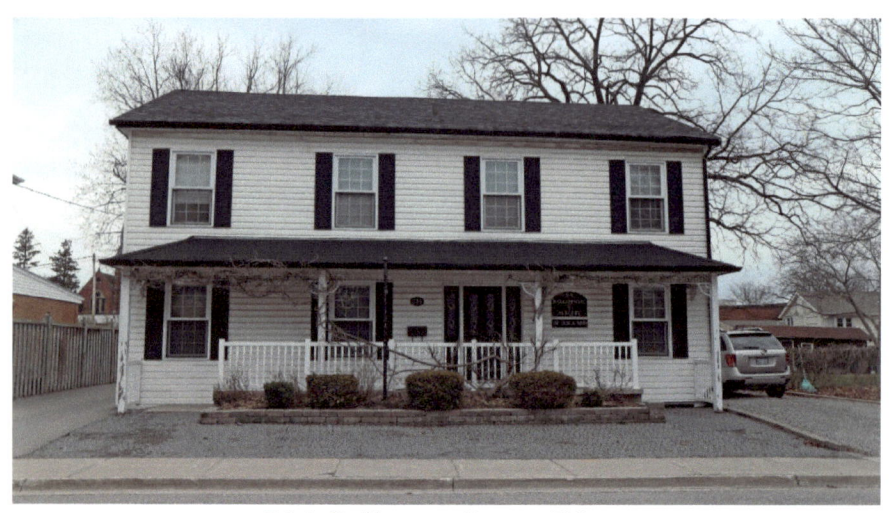

214 Colborne Street West

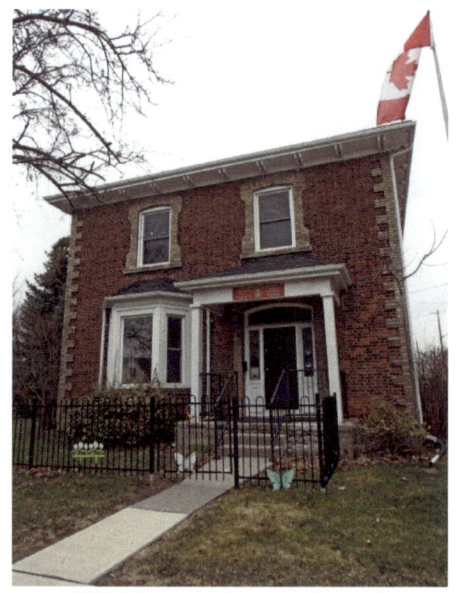

200 Byron Street South

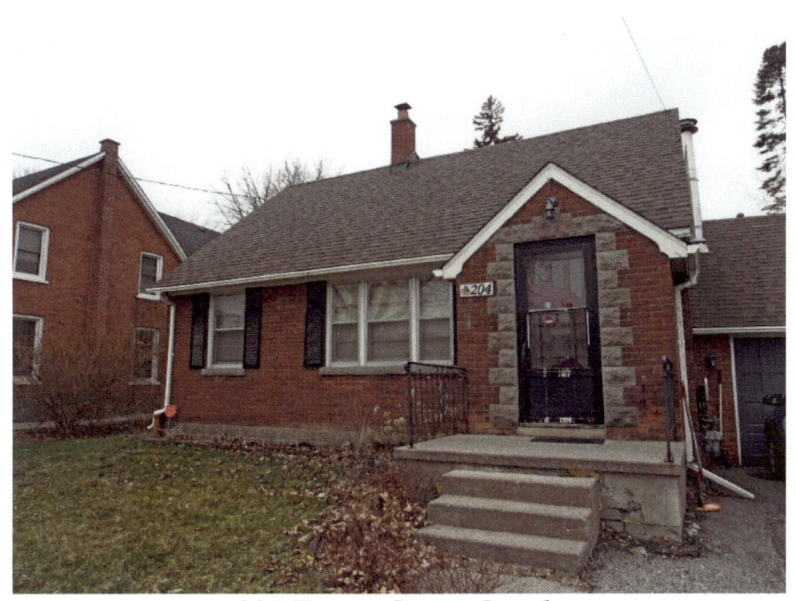

204 Byron Street South

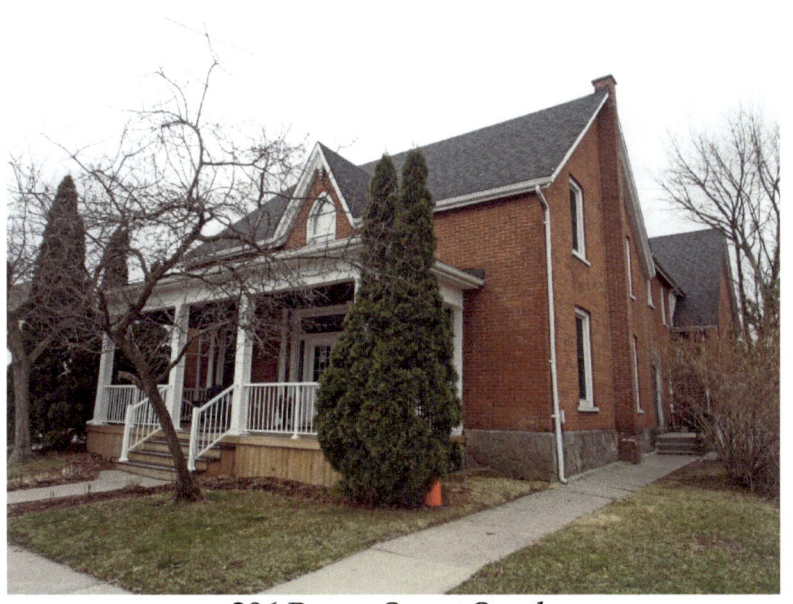

206 Byron Street South

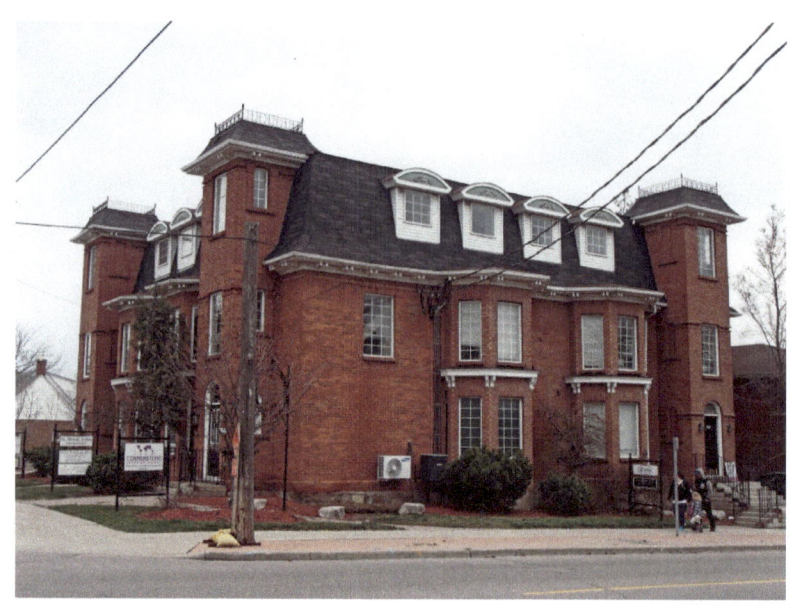

213 Byron Street South/101 Dunlop Street West

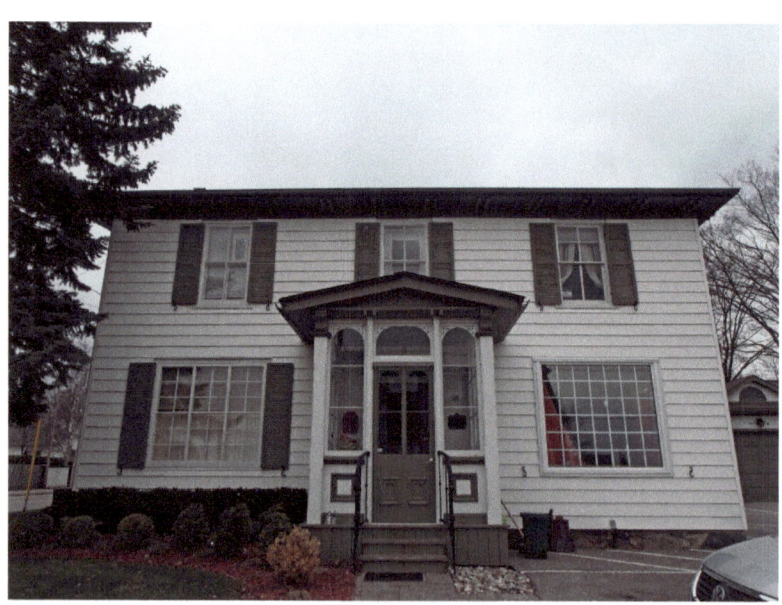

208 Byron Street South – built in 1868 – All Saints Rectory from 1882 to 1951 – tongue-in-groove frame house

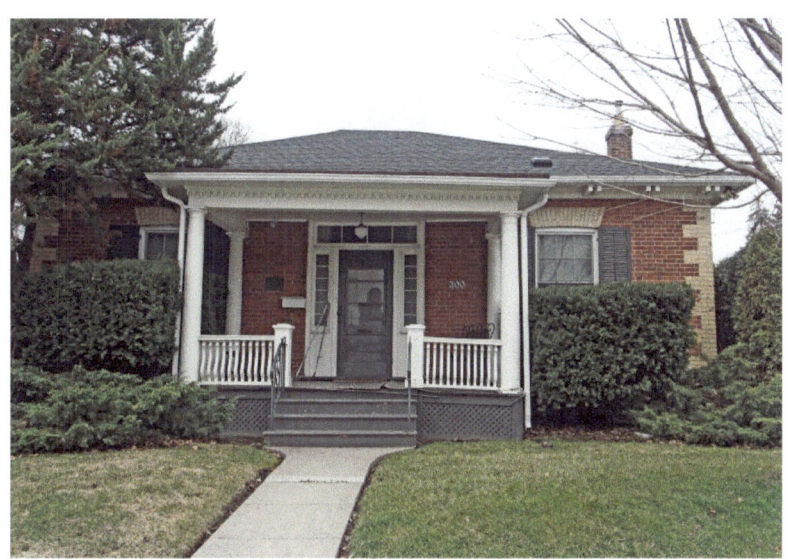

300 Byron Street South – Jacob Bryan House – c. 1862

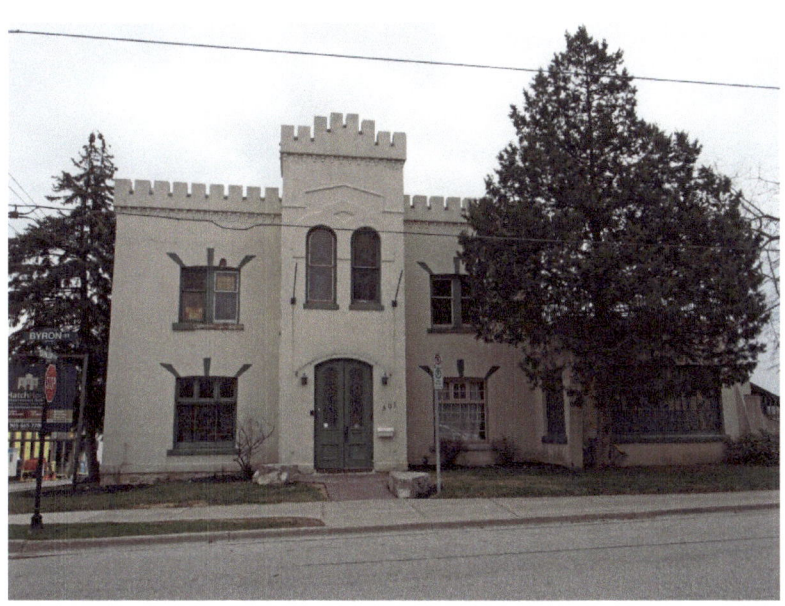

301 Byron Street South

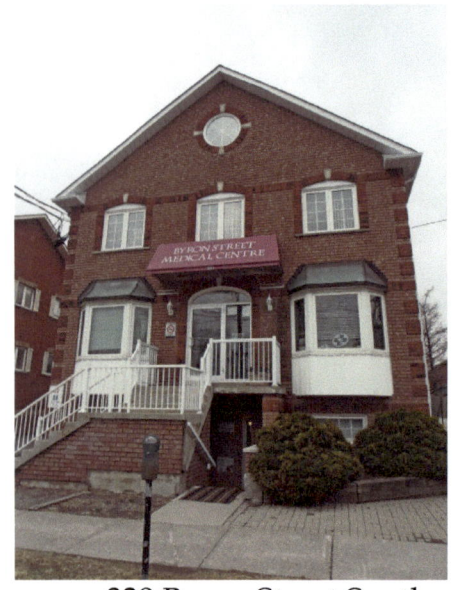
320 Byron Street South

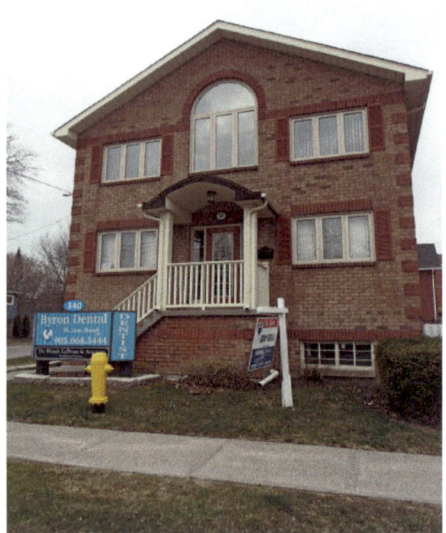
340 Byron Street South

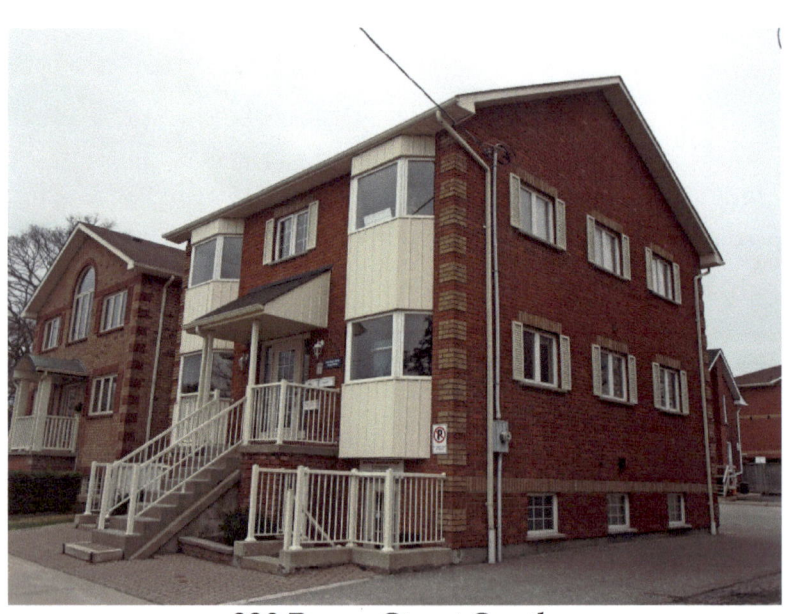
330 Byron Street South

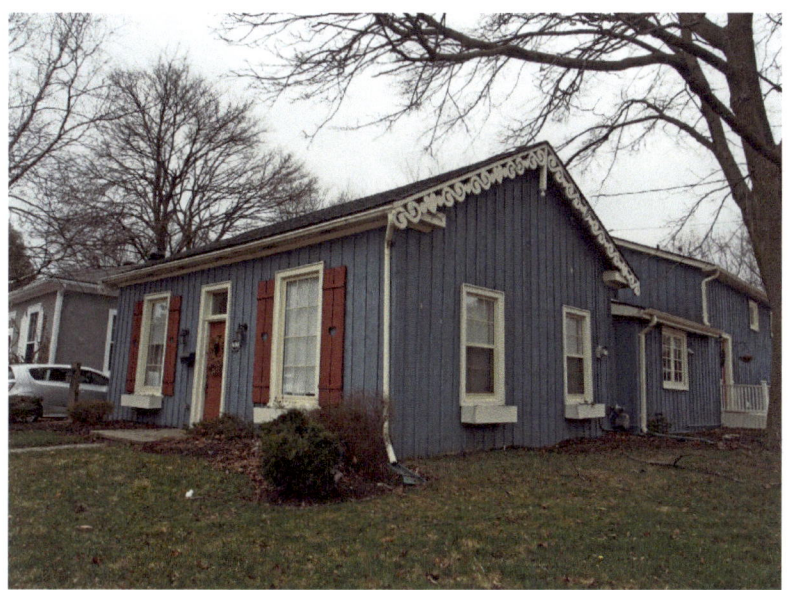

400 Byron Street South

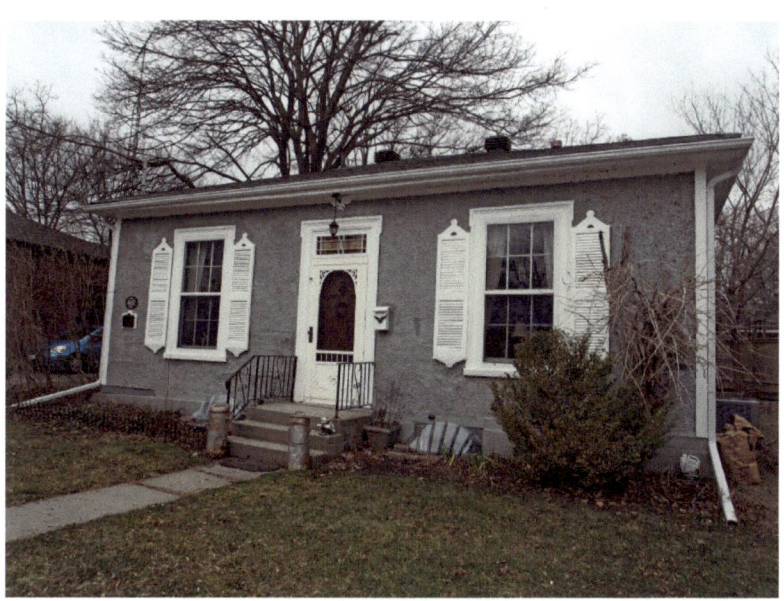

402 Byron Street South – Adams-Beckham House – c. 1853 - Ontario Vernacular Cottage design

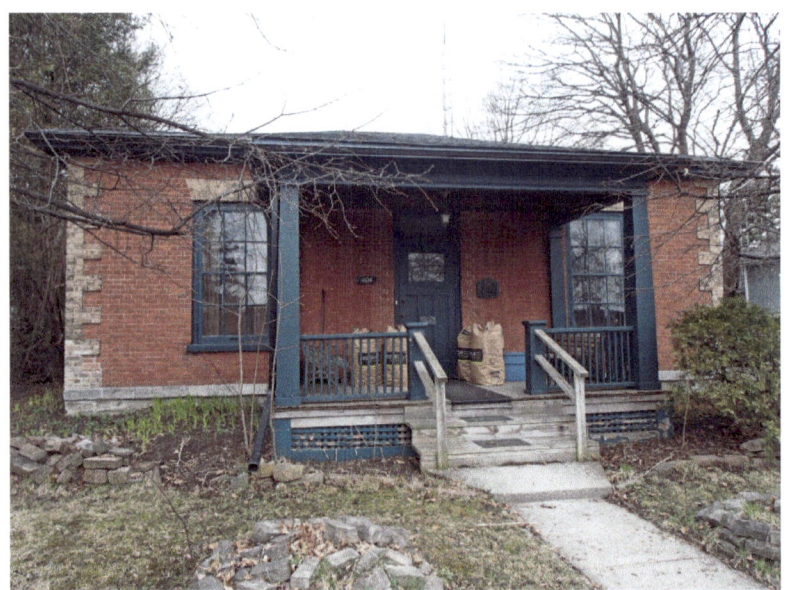

404 Byron Street South – George Wallace (merchant and town councillor) House - circa 1853 - Ontario Vernacular Cottage design built

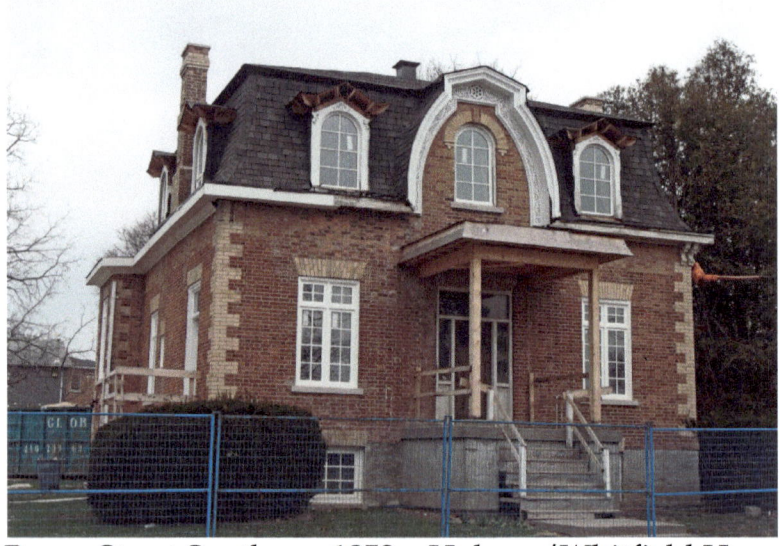

408 Byron Street South – c. 1853 – Holmes/Whitfield House - Second Empire style with mansard roof added about 1875

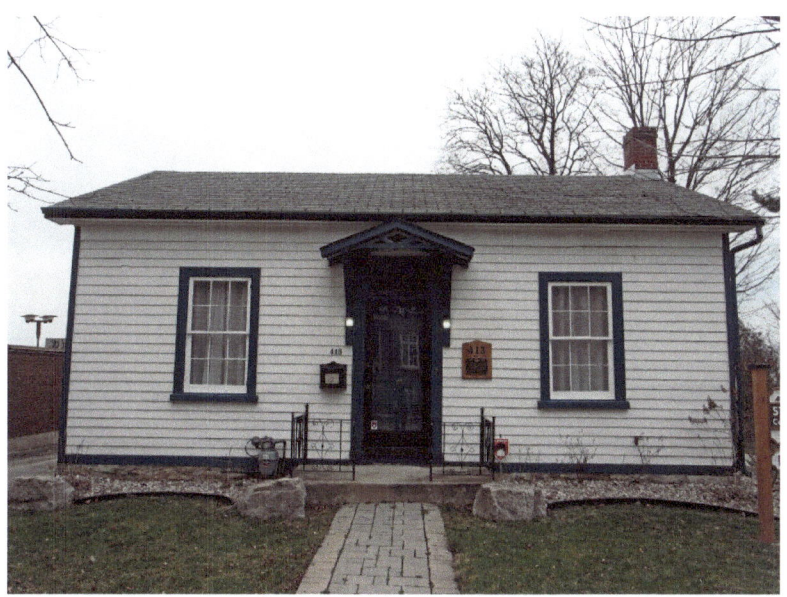

413 Byron Street – William Carpenter House - circa 1854 – three-bay, story-and-a-half, T-form clapboard house

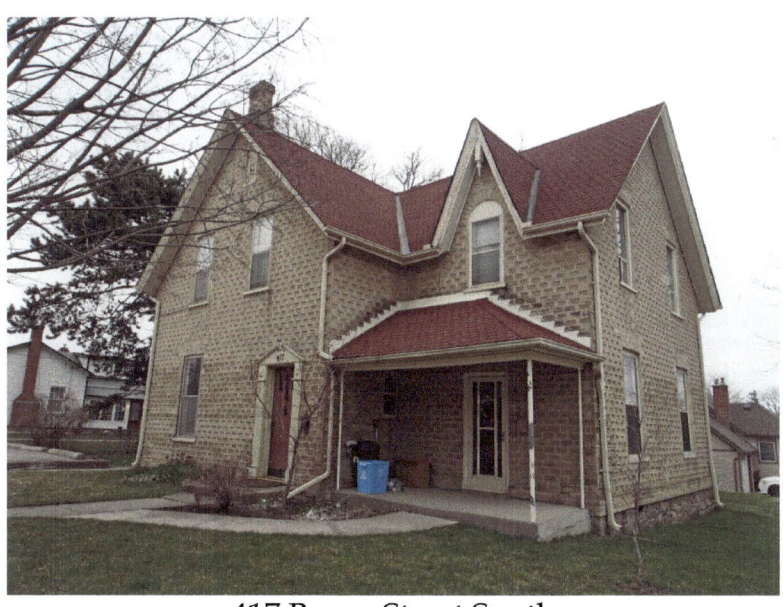

417 Byron Street South

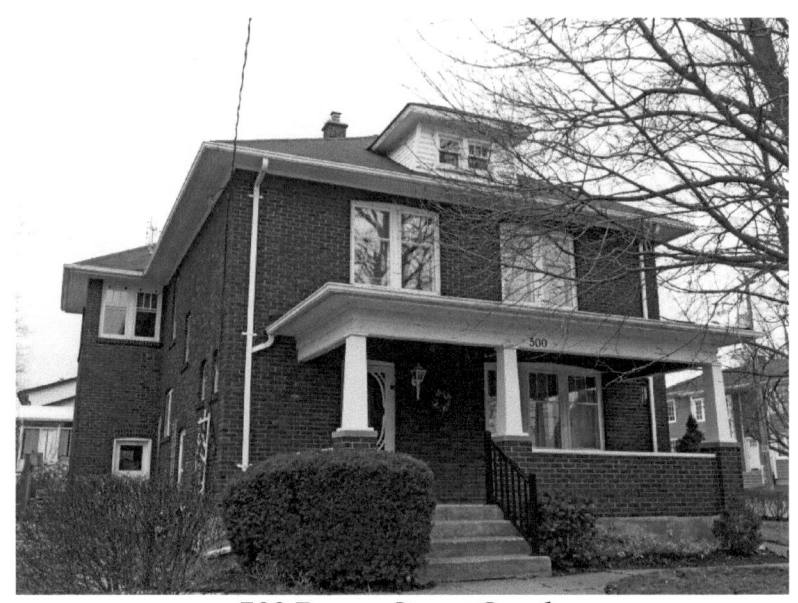

500 Byron Street South

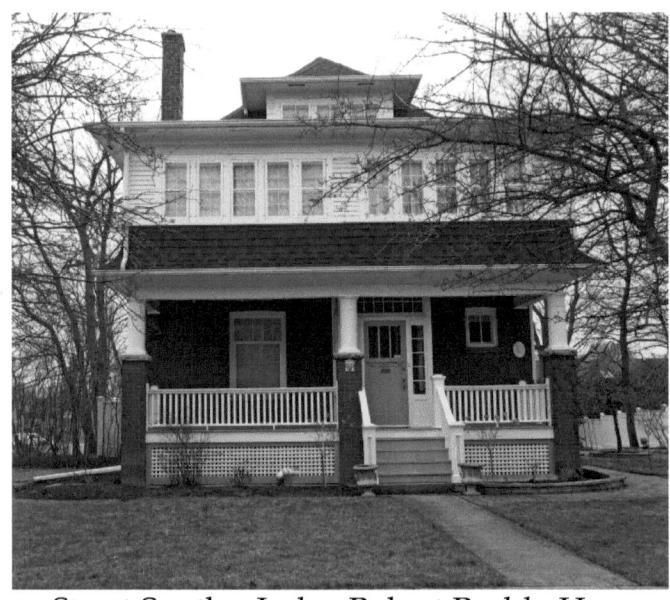

501 Byron Street South – Judge Robert Ruddy House – c. 1915

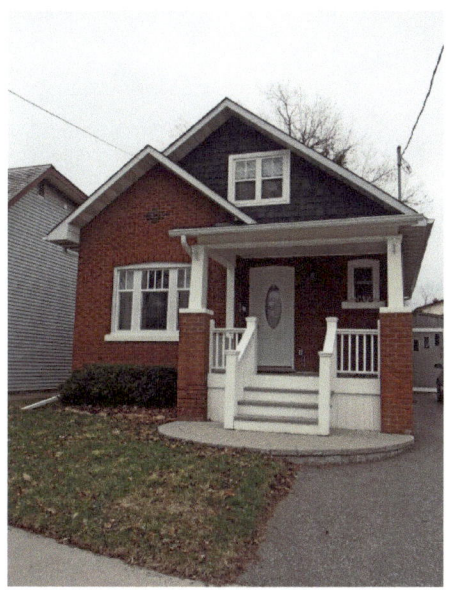

502 Byron Street South

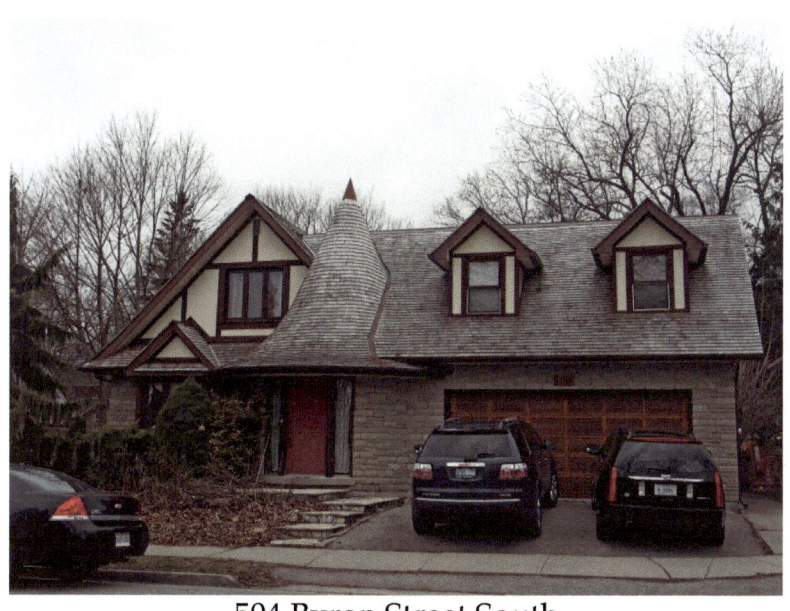

504 Byron Street South

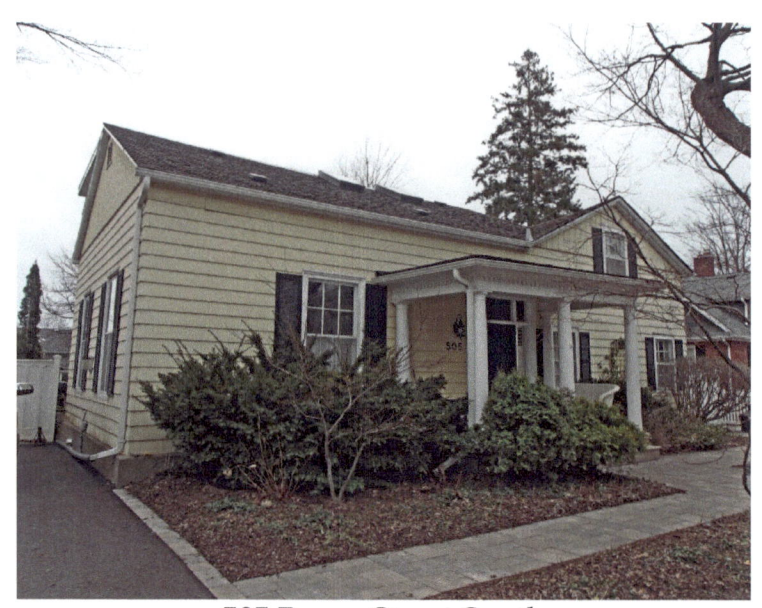

505 Byron Street South

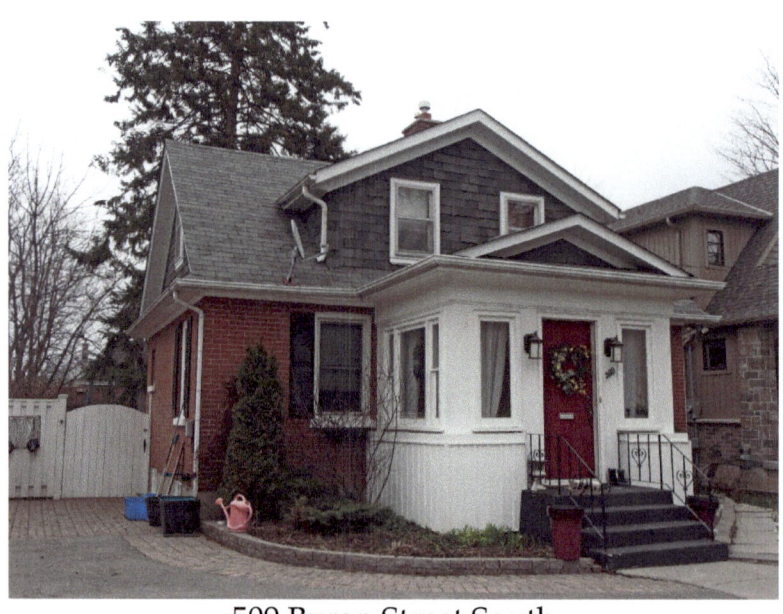

509 Byron Street South

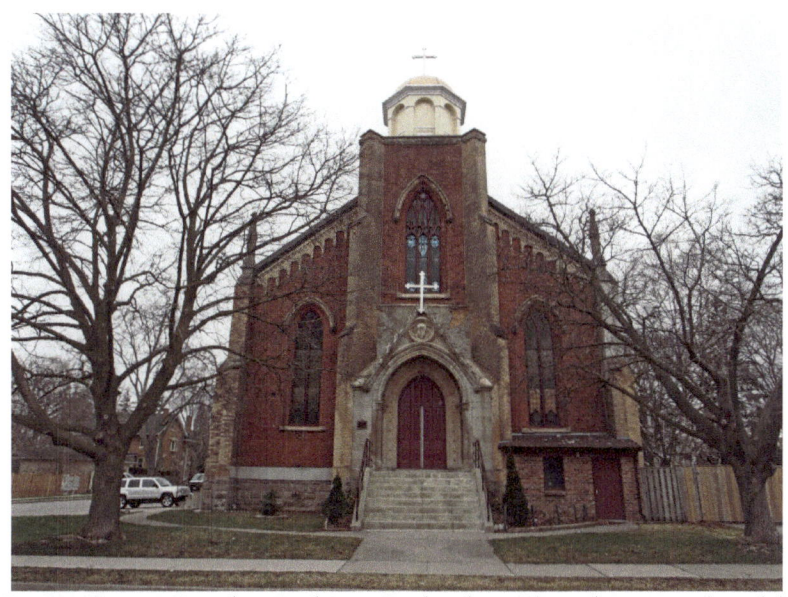

508 Byron Street South - Serbian Orthodox Church – cupola added in 2012 – Gothic Revival (formerly St. Andrew's Presbyterian Church 1857-1968) – The face carved over the front door is that of John Knox, the founder of Presbyterianism.

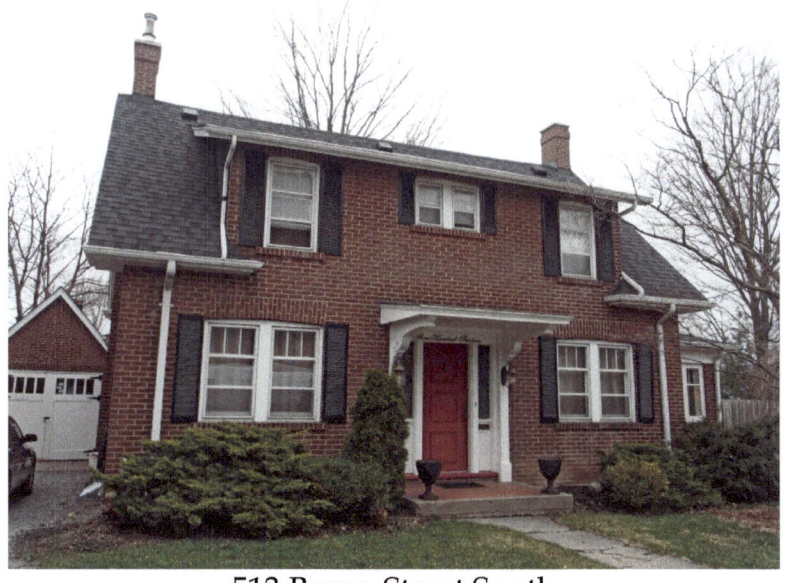

513 Byron Street South

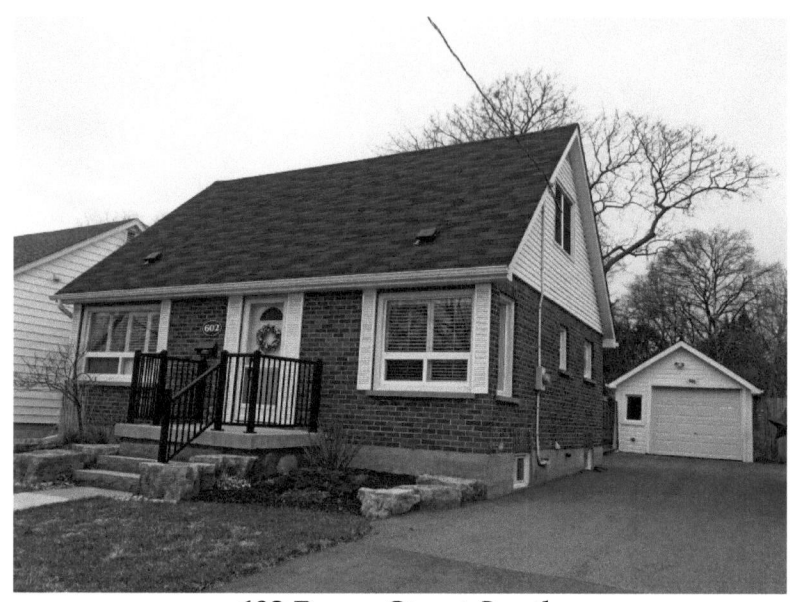
602 Byron Street South

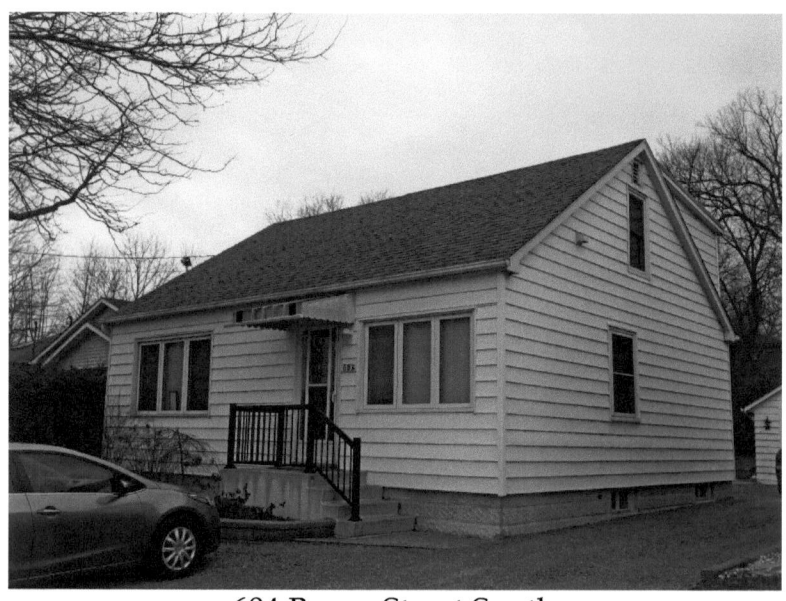
604 Byron Street South

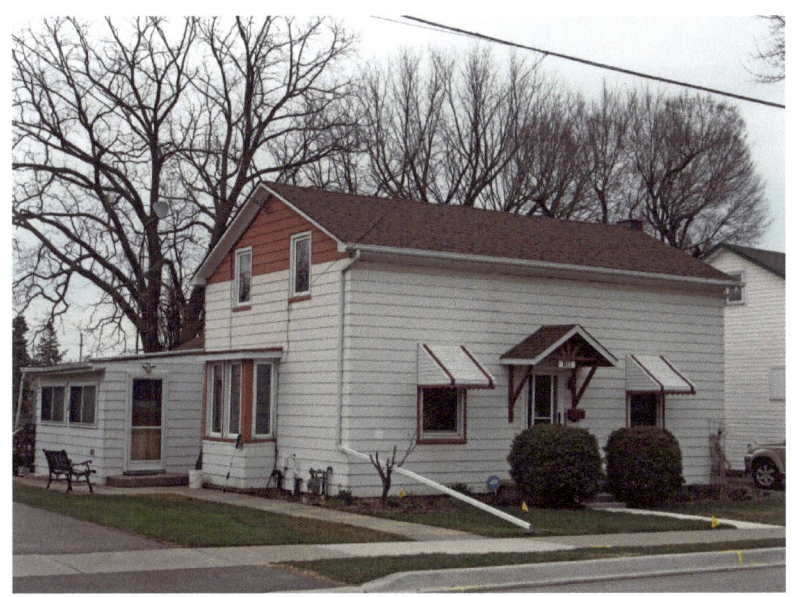

611 Byron Street South

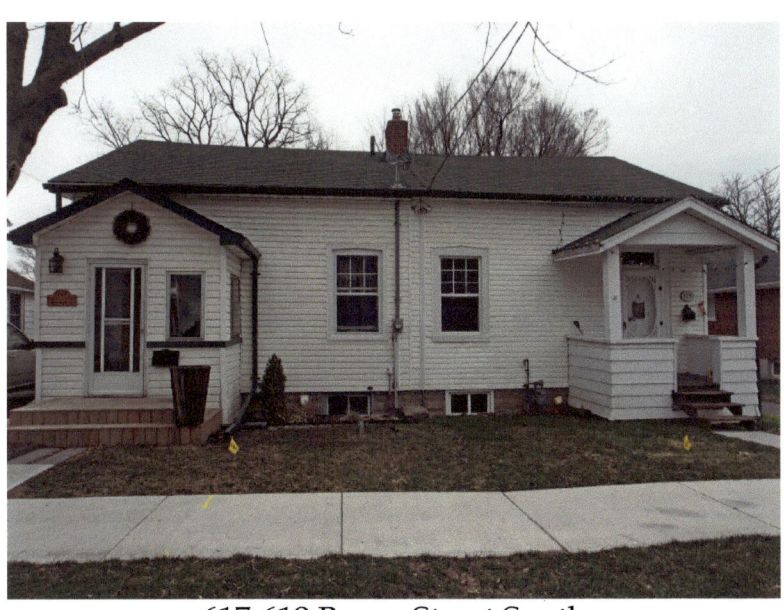

617-619 Byron Street South

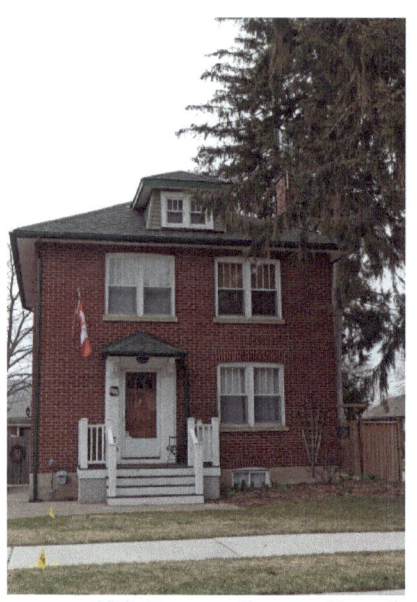
629 Byron Street South

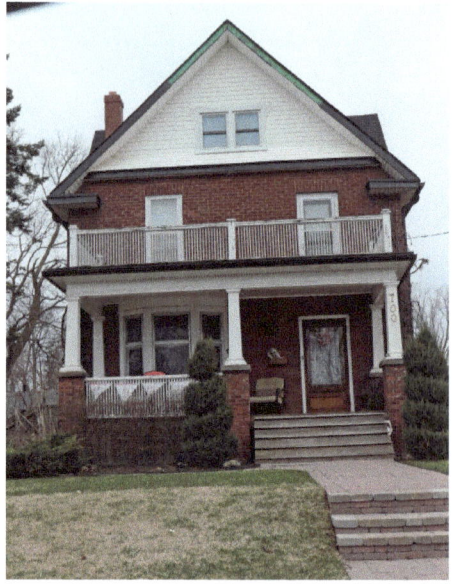
700 Byron Street South
Charles Ryecroft House - 1905

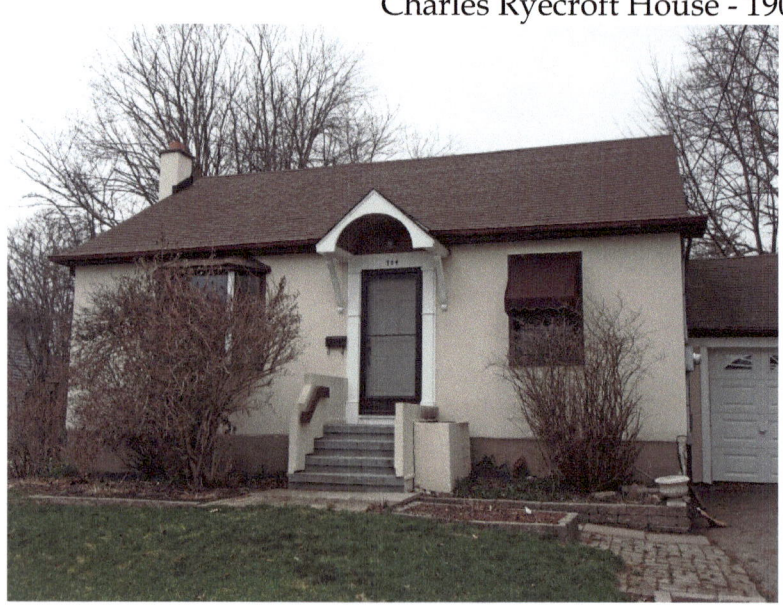
704 Byron Street South

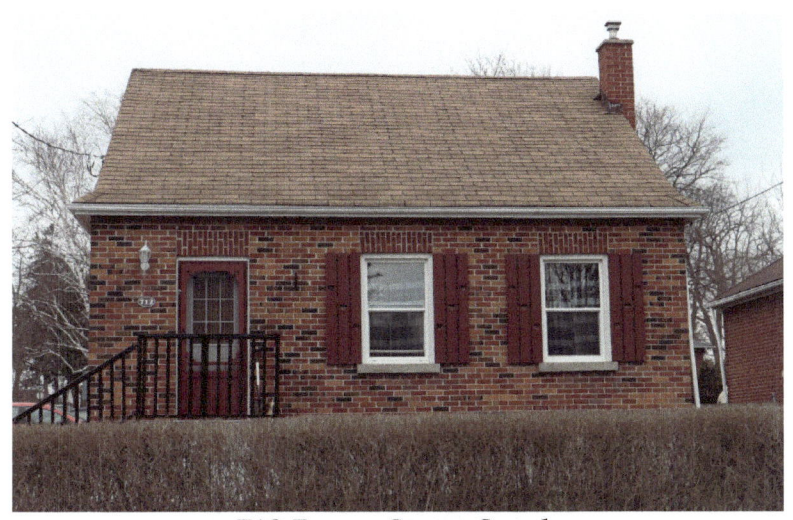

712 Byron Street South

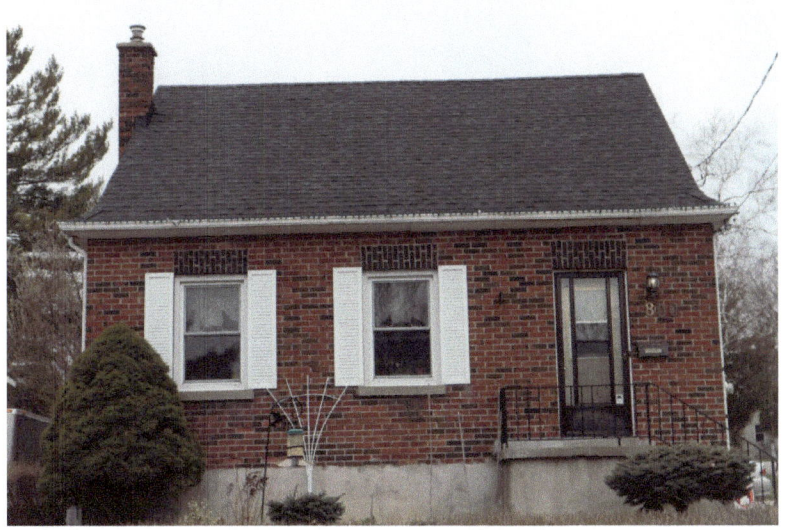

800 Byron Street South

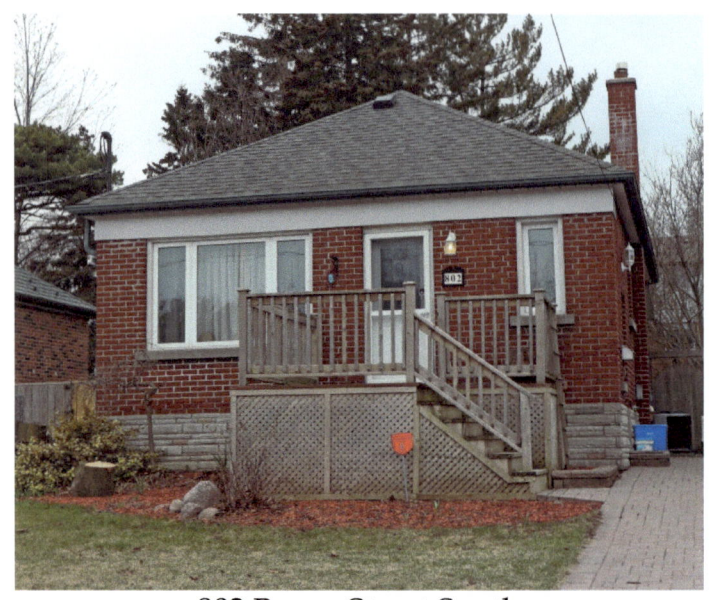

802 Byron Street South

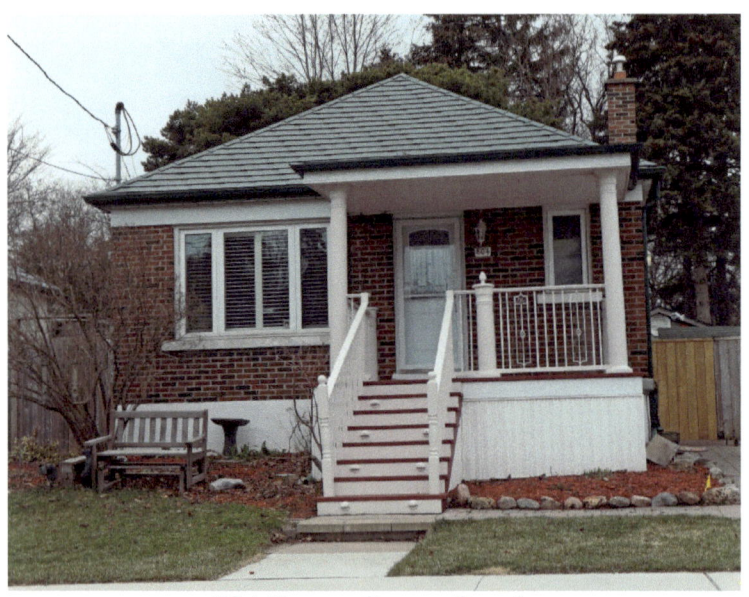

804 Byron Street South

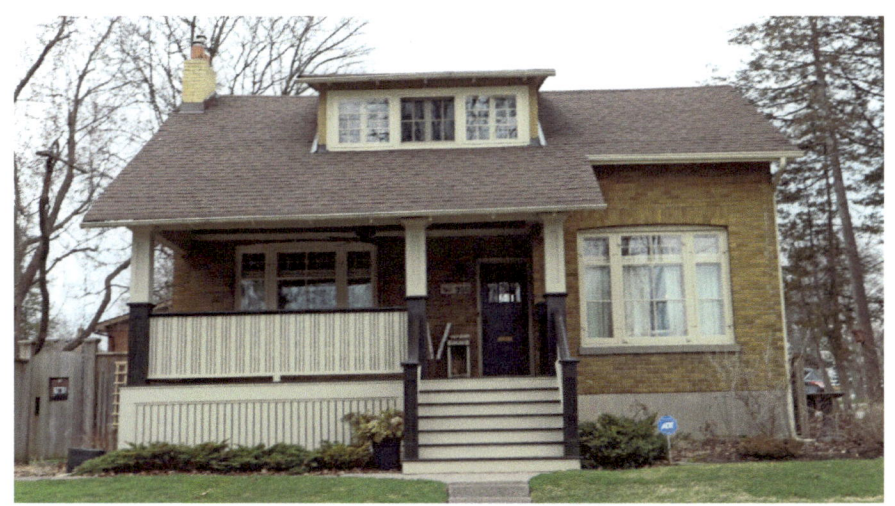

900 Byron Street South

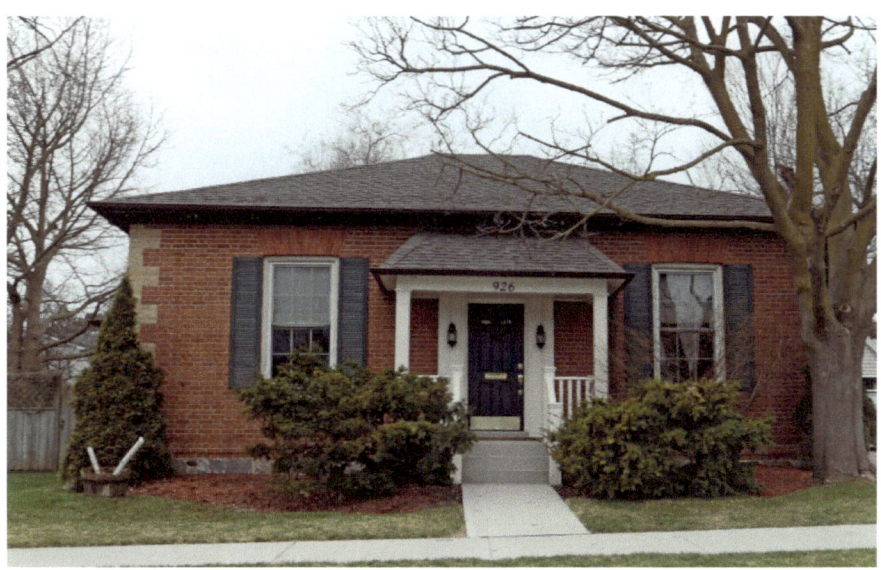

926 Byron Street South – James Keith Gordon House - 1853

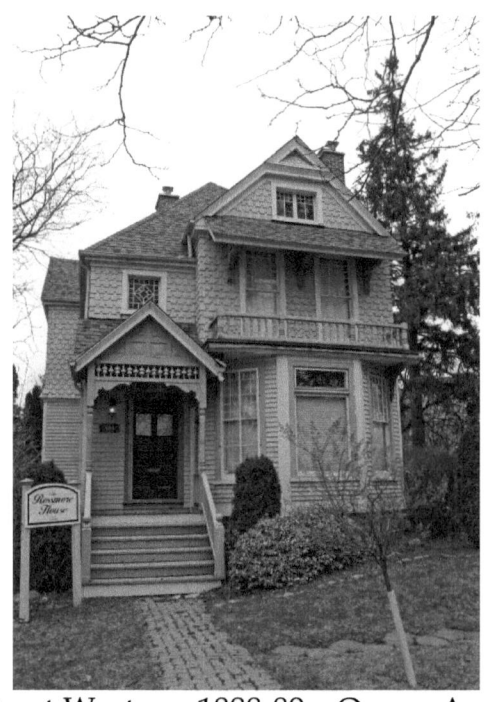

404 Dunlop Street West – c. 1888-89 – Queen Anne Revival style – asymmetrical design – built for George Ross – Mrs. Ross was president of Whitby Women's Institute and founder of the Victorian Order of Nurses in Ontario County.

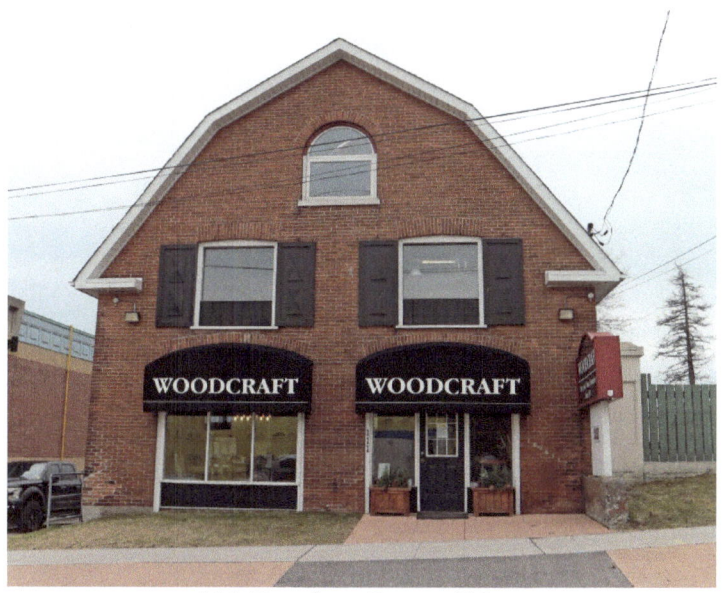

111 Dunlop Street West

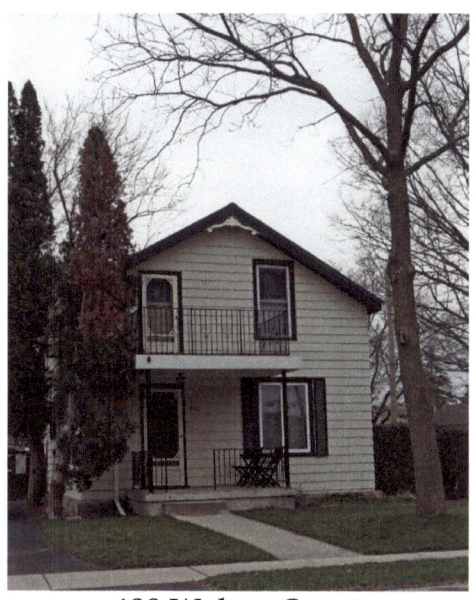

400 Walnut Street

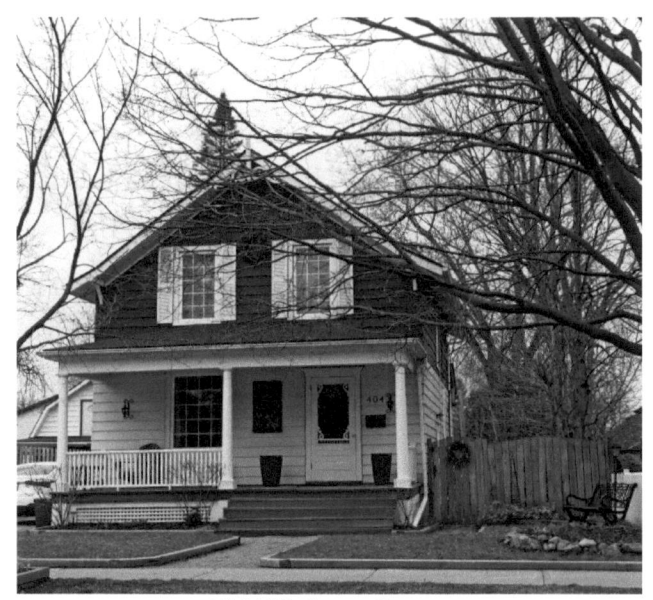

404 Walnut Street

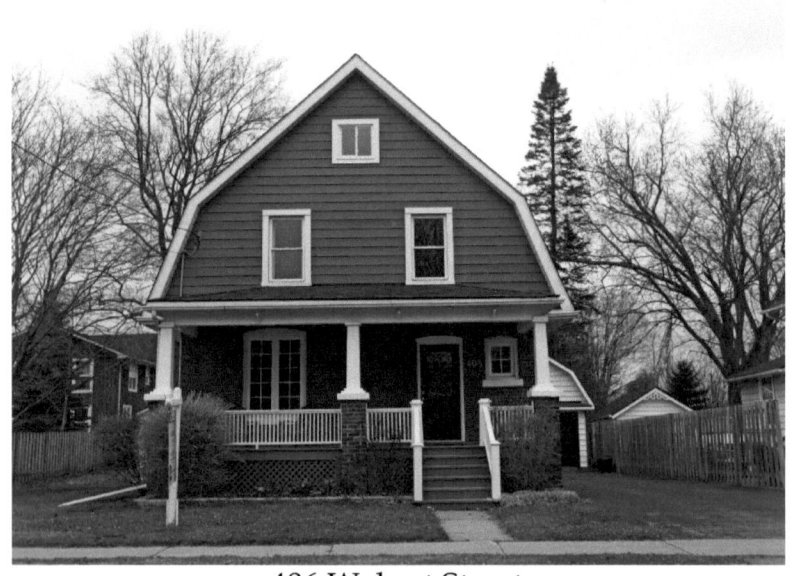

406 Walnut Street

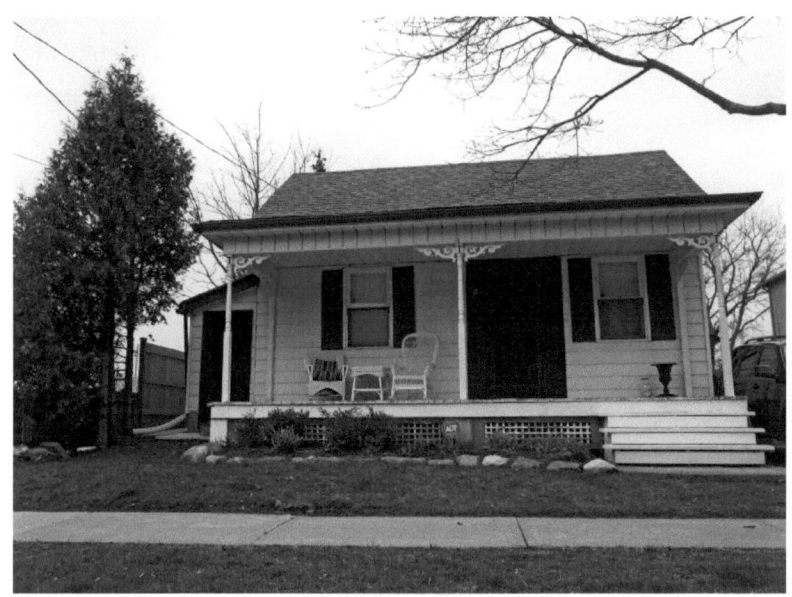

Walnut Street

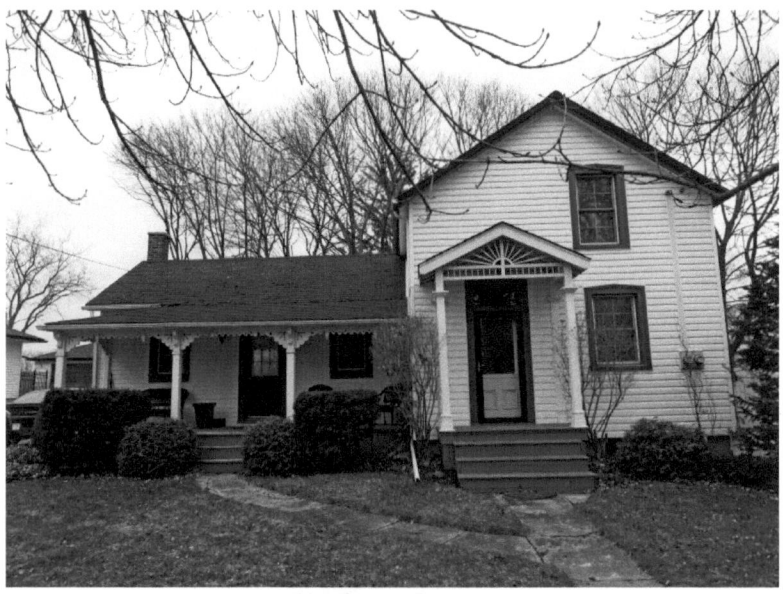

Walnut Street

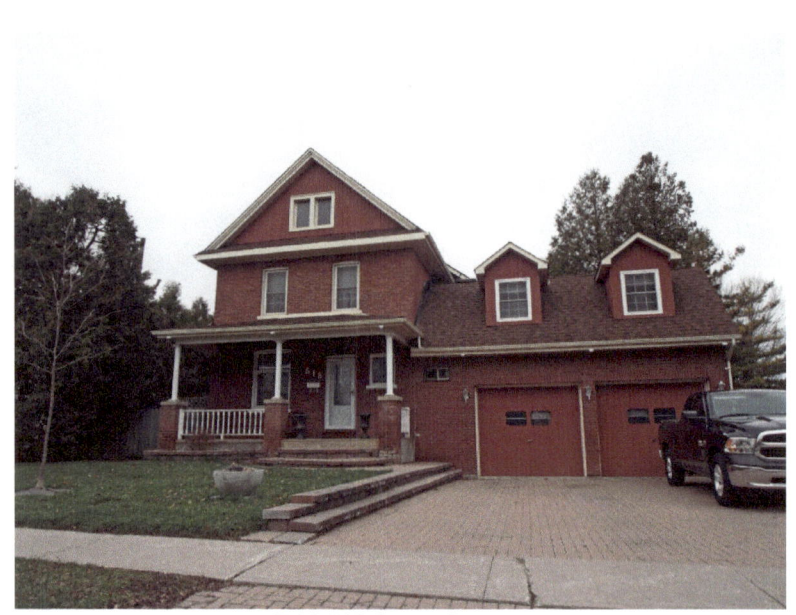

518 Walnut Street

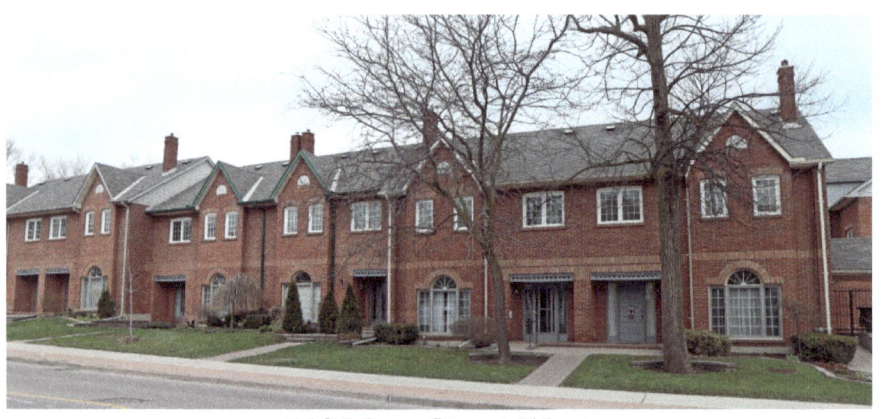

110 Mary Street West

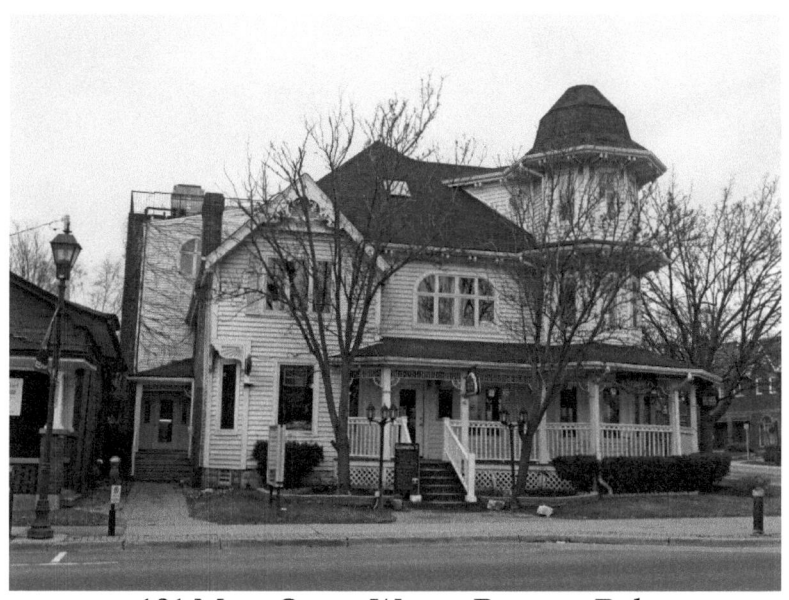

101 Mary Street West – Pearson Pub

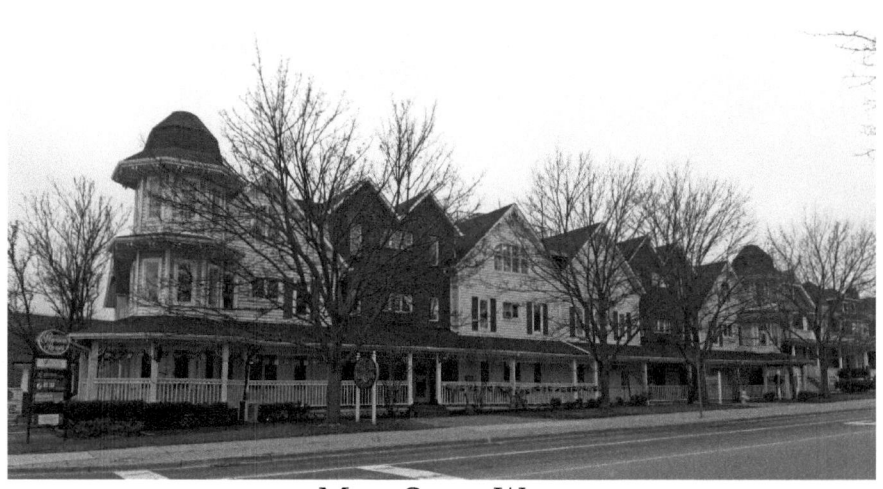

Mary Street West

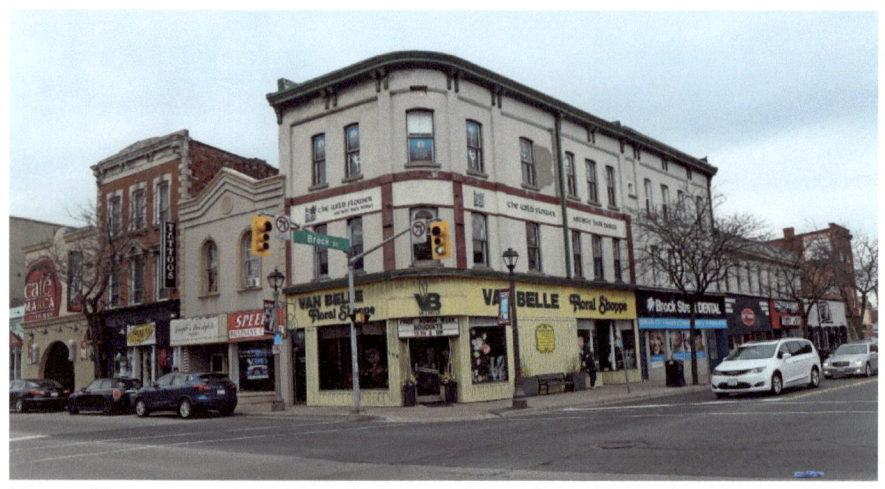

Four Corners – 100 Brock Street North at Dundas Street West
100-108 Brock Street North – c. 1873 – The James H. Gerrie Block was originally a drugstore and served that purpose for ninety-six years. It was originally built of red brick but was stuccoed over in 1939.

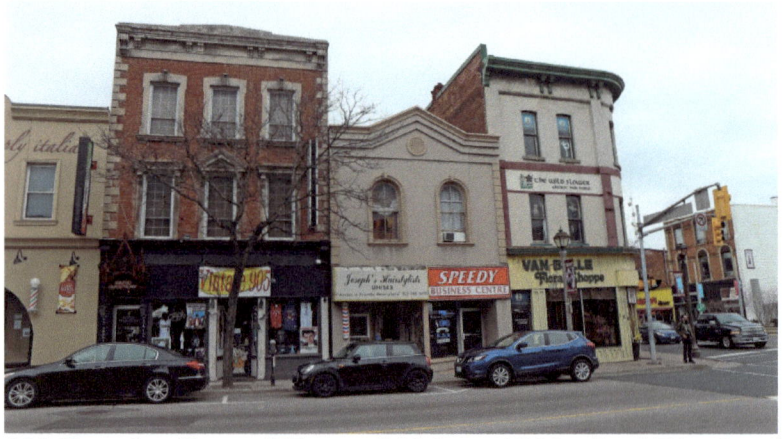

100-108 Dundas Street West – #106 - c. 1860 – Joel Bigelow's Block – Renaissance Revival style

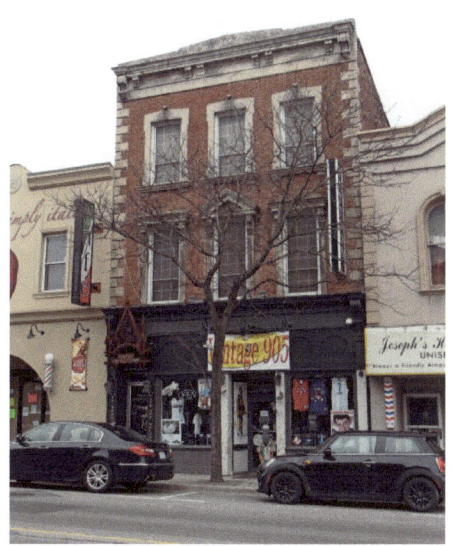

108 Dundas Street West

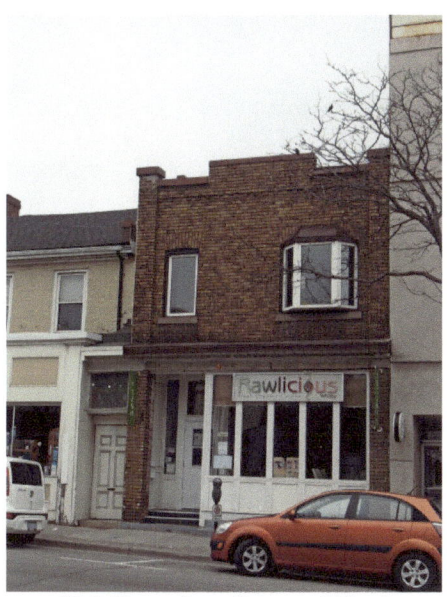

120 Dundas Street West

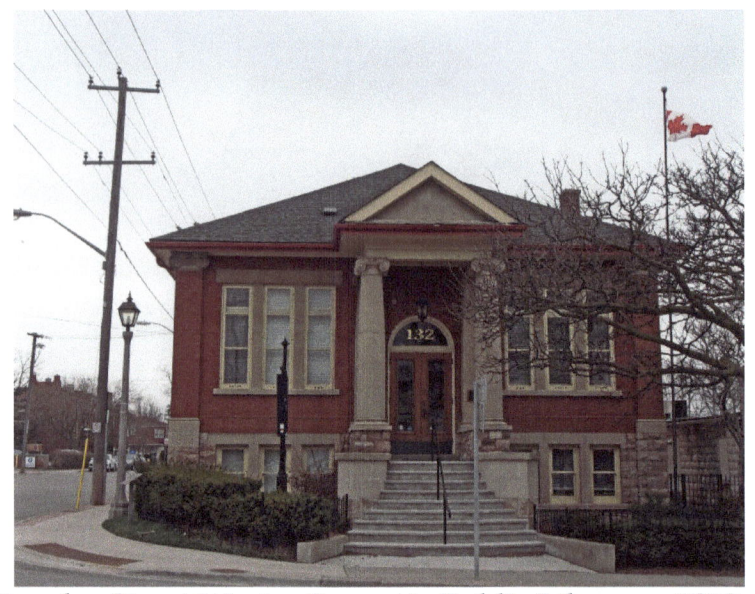

132 Dundas Street West – Carnegie Public Library – 1913 – closed as a library in 1973

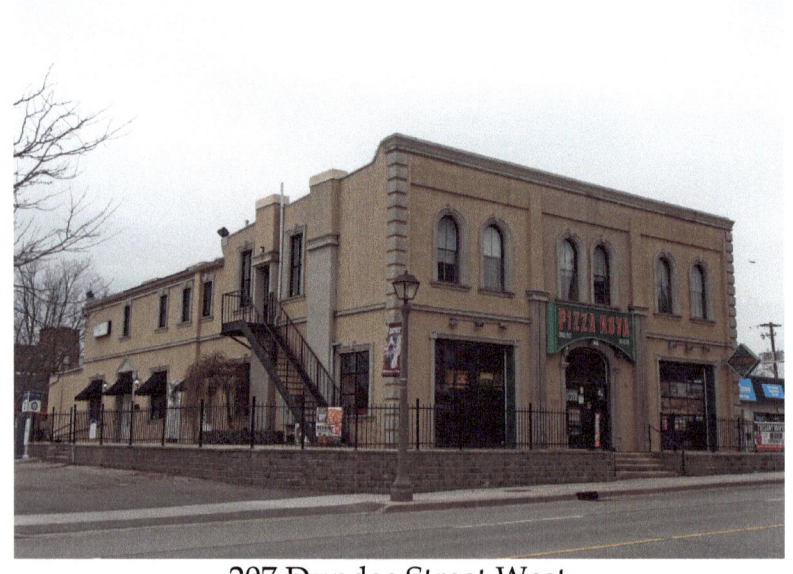

207 Dundas Street West

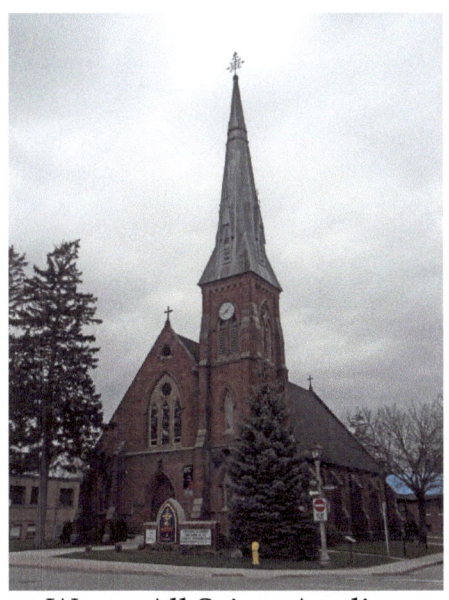

300 Dundas Street West - All Saints Anglican – c. 1865-66 – Gothic Revival – spire added in 1870

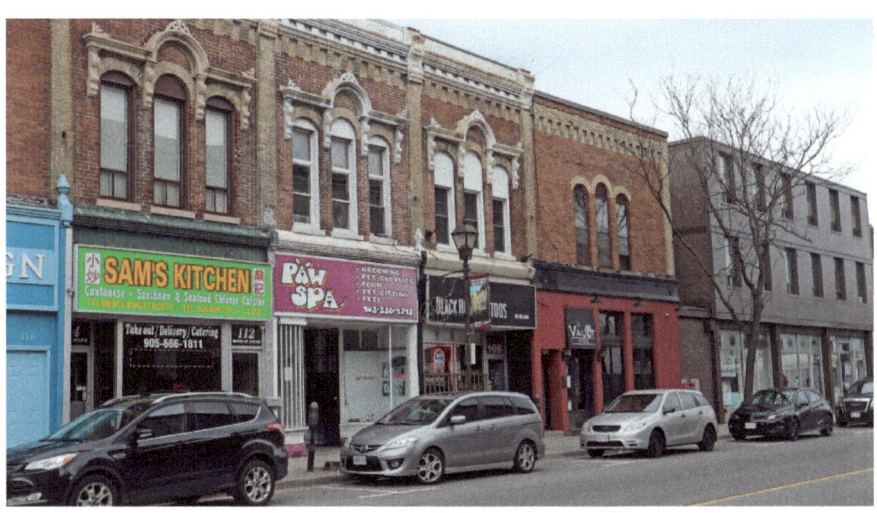

101-114 Brock Street South

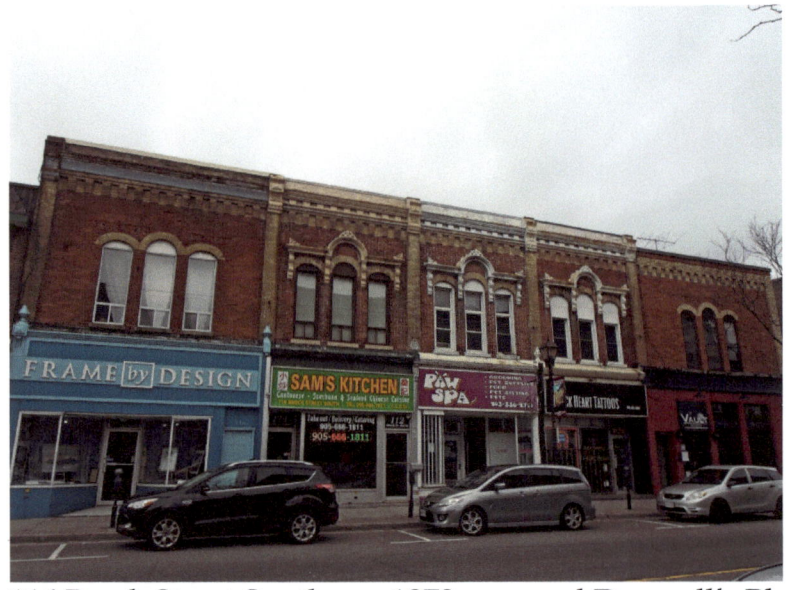

104-116 Brock Street South – c. 1878 – named Deverell's Block after its builder, Thomas Deverell, contractor – from 1900-1917 it was the Windsor Hotel, and then it was reverted to stores

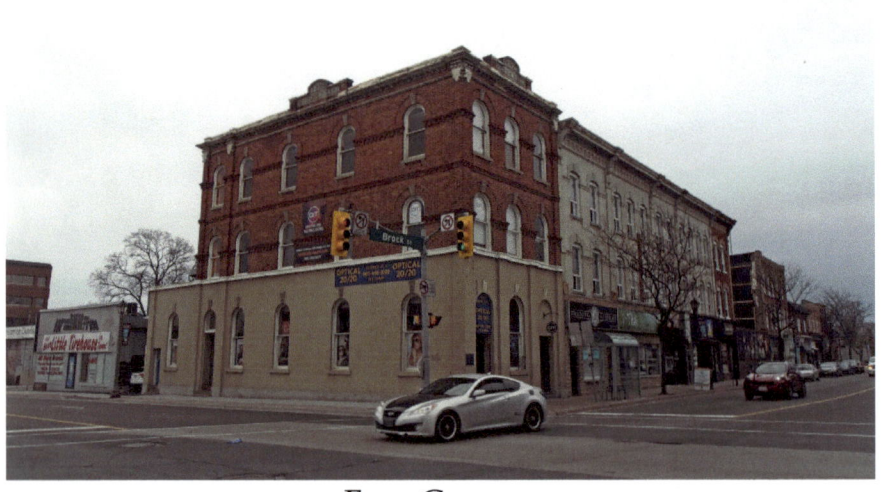

Four Corners

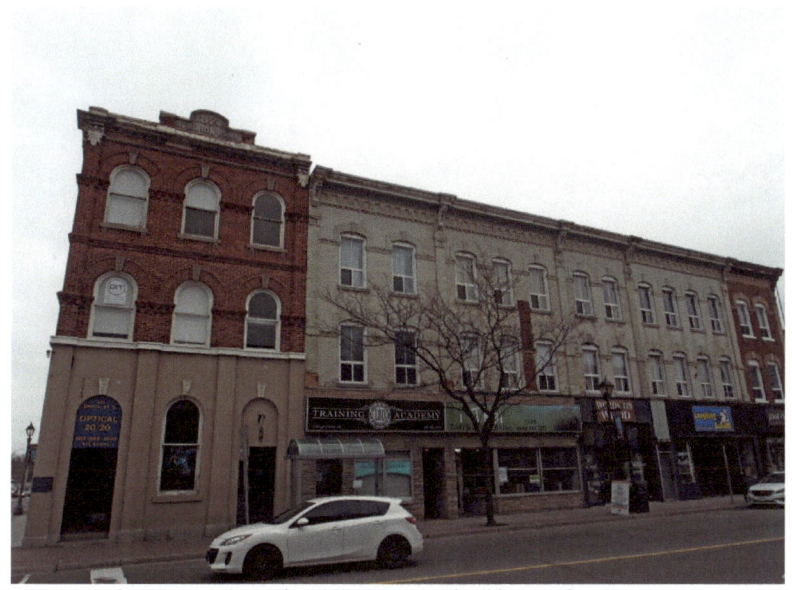

101-113 Brock Street South - #101 was built as the Dominion Bank c. 1874 – It was the only building in this block to survive the great fire of October 16, 1877. #103-113 – 1878 – Watson's Block

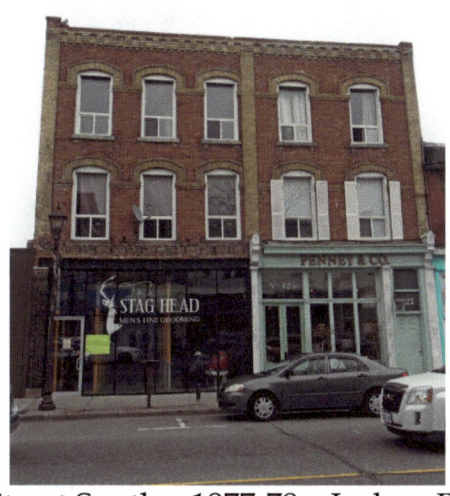

123-127 Brock Street South – 1877-78 – Joshua Richardson Block

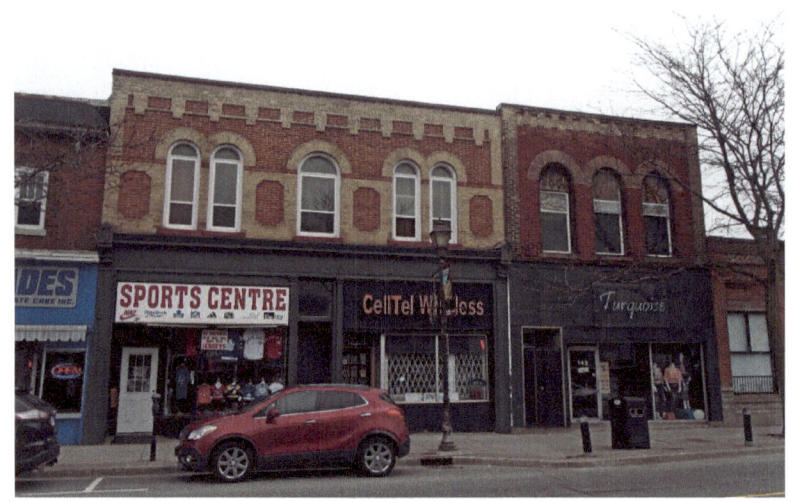

137-141 Brock Street South – 1880-81
143 Brock Street South – Till Block - 1879

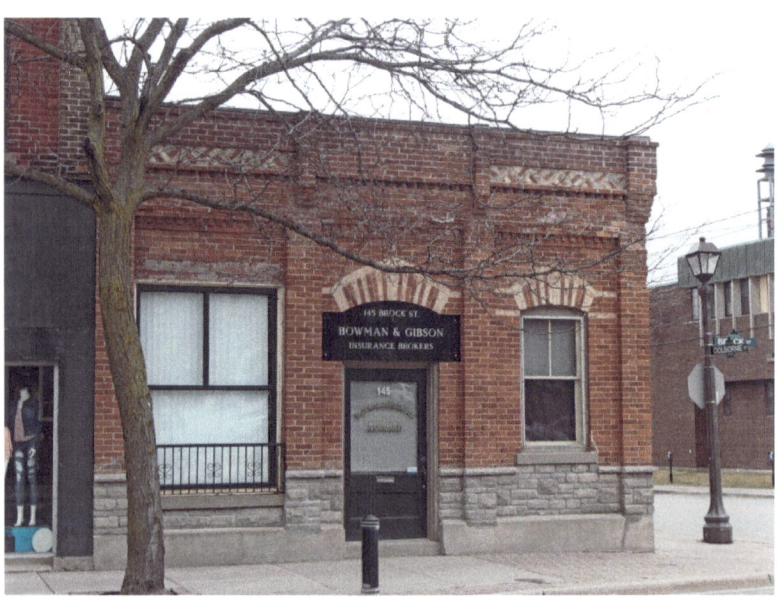

145 Brock Street South

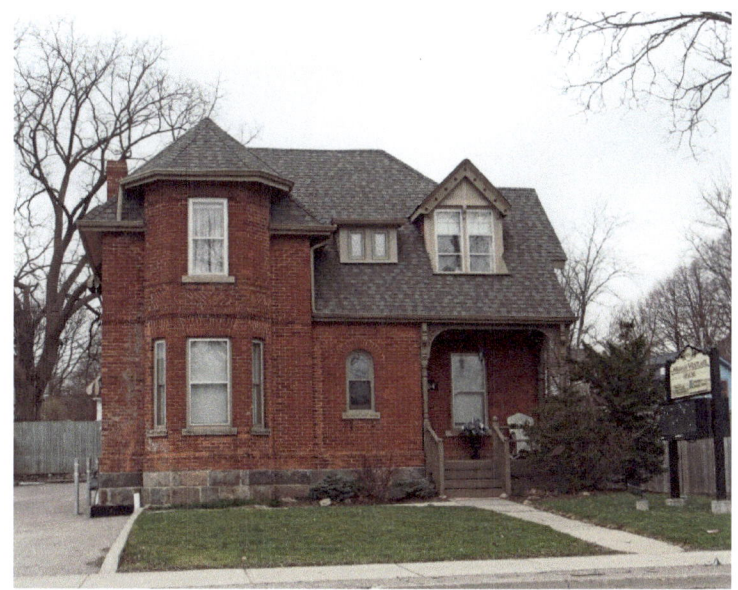

604 Brock Street South – William Westlake House – c. 1877

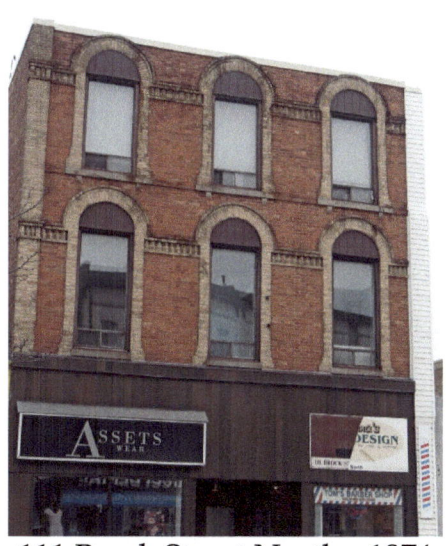

111 Brock Street North - 1874

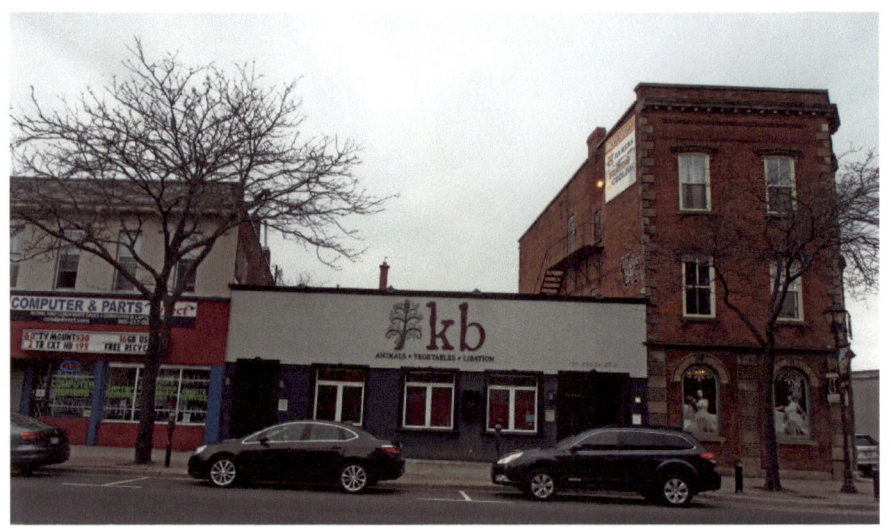
120 Brock Street North

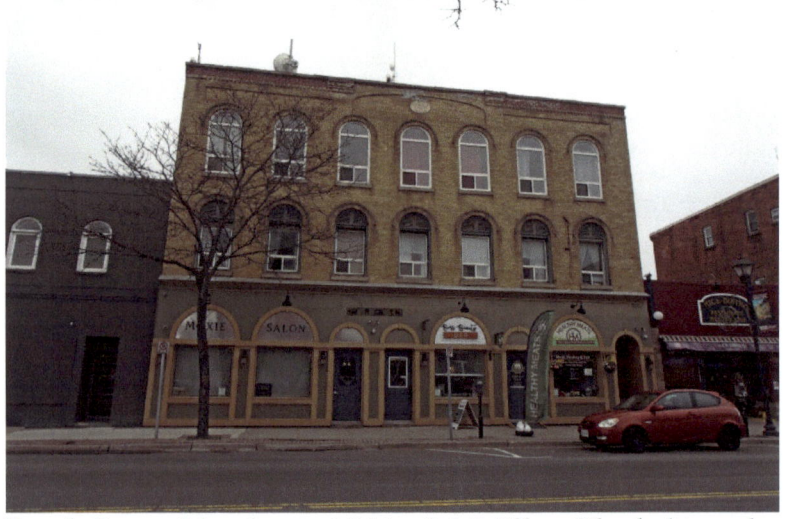
121 Brock Street North – c. 1864 – McMillan Block (it replaced Perry's Block which burned down in June 1864) – The centre of the three stores was occupied by the offices of the Royal Canadian Bank, the Dominion Bank, and the Western Bank of Canada. The north store served as Whitby's Post Office from 1880-1910.

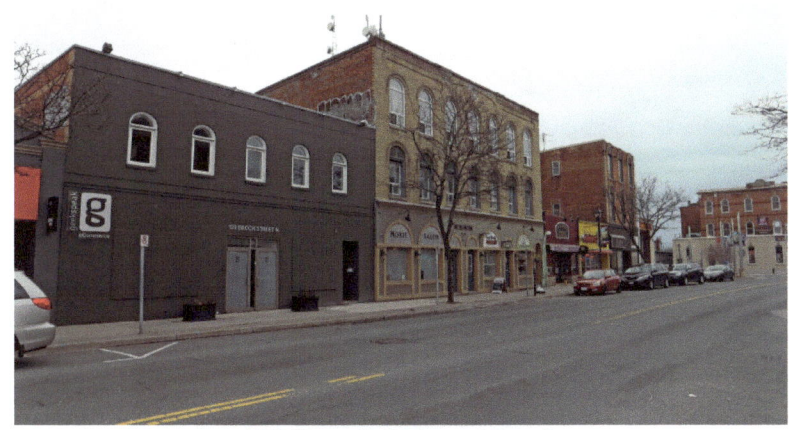

129 Brock Street North

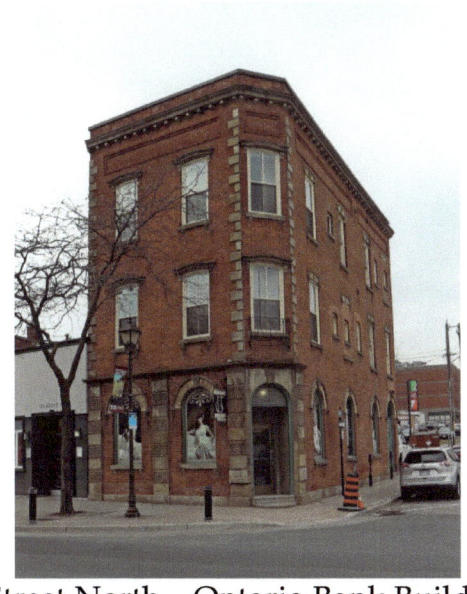

122 Brock Street North – Ontario Bank Building - c. 1867

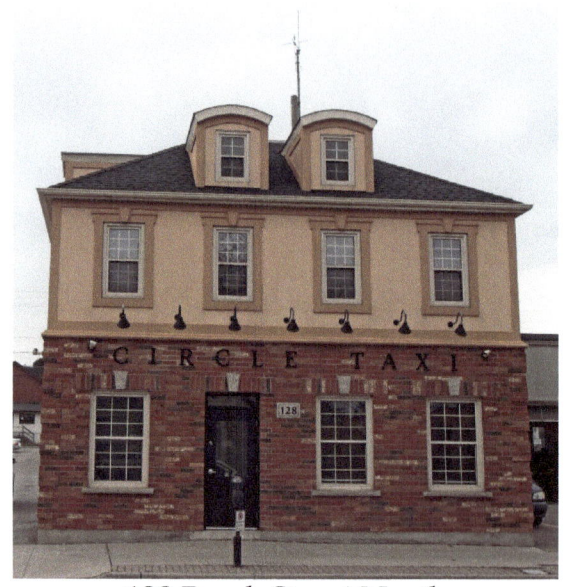

128 Brock Street North

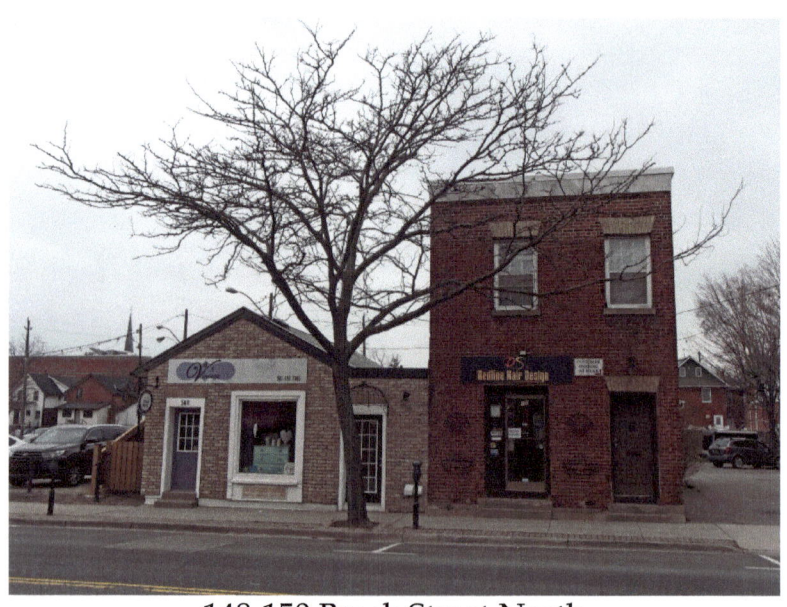

148-150 Brock Street North

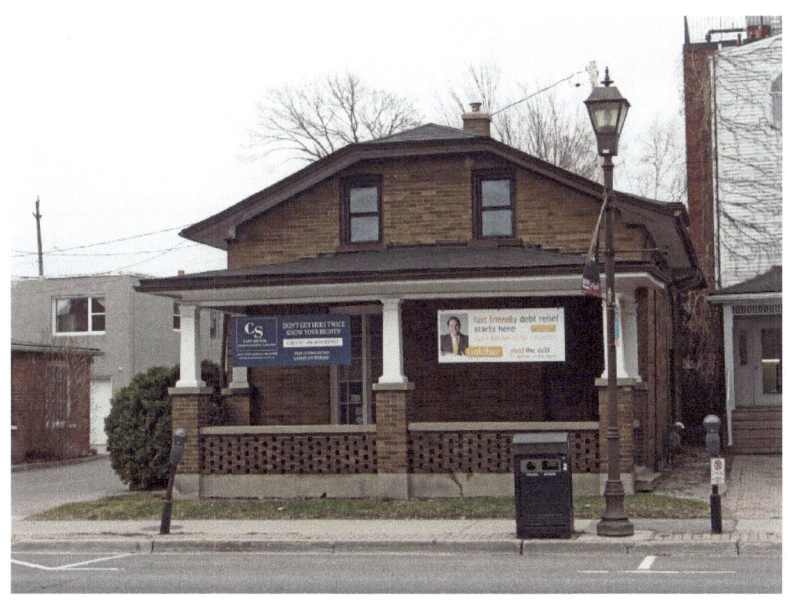

Brock Street North

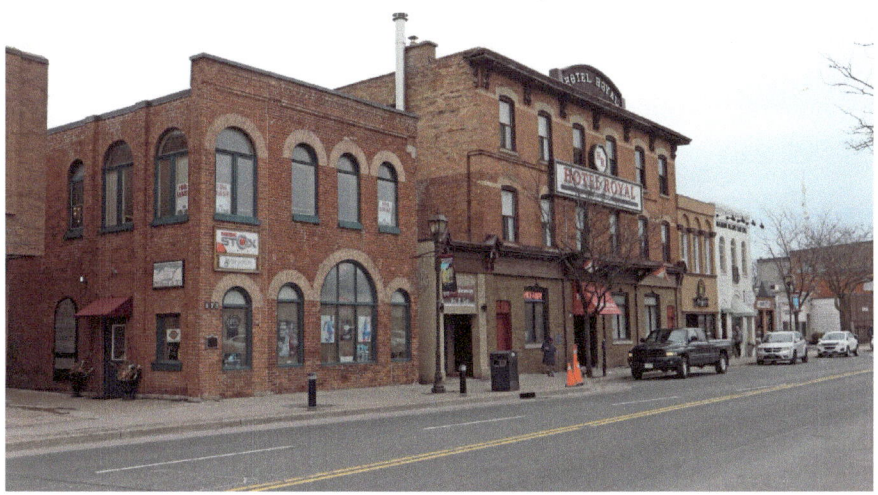

173 Brock Street North – c. 1862 – known as the Whitby Chronicle Building as it was originally the office of W.H. Higgins, publisher of the Whitby Chronicle.

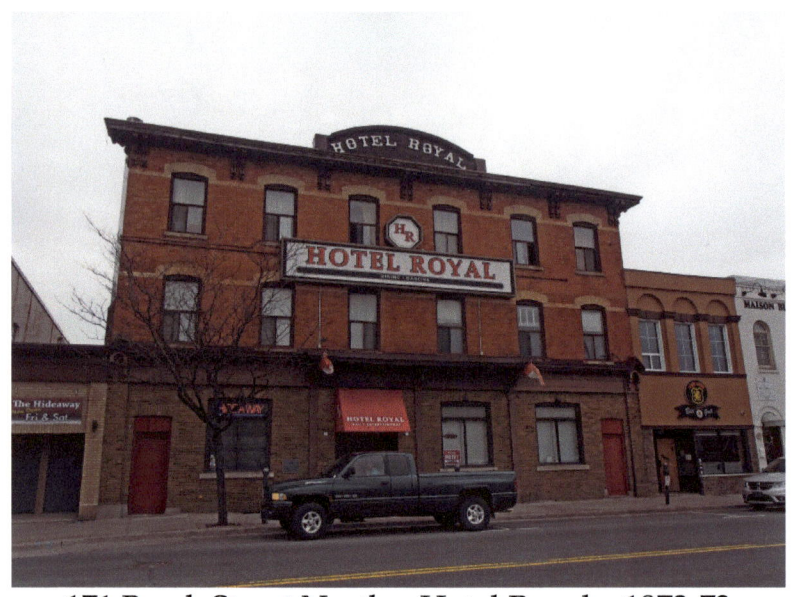

171 Brock Street North – Hotel Royal – 1872-73

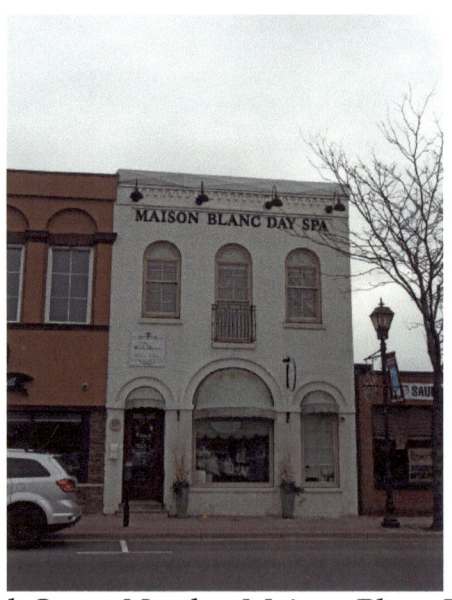

159 Brock Street North – Maison Blanc Day Spa

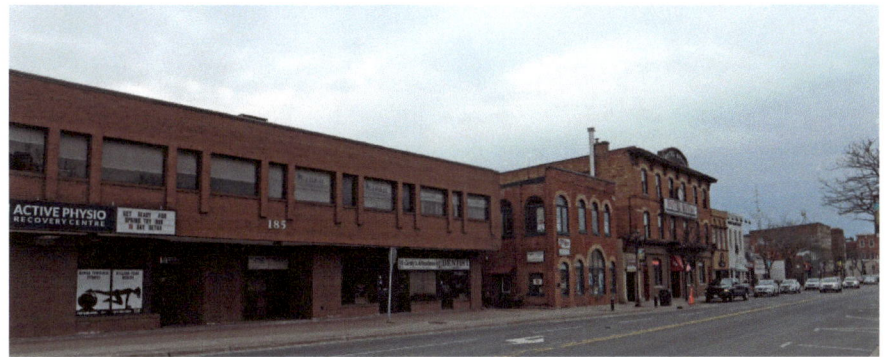
185 Brock Street North

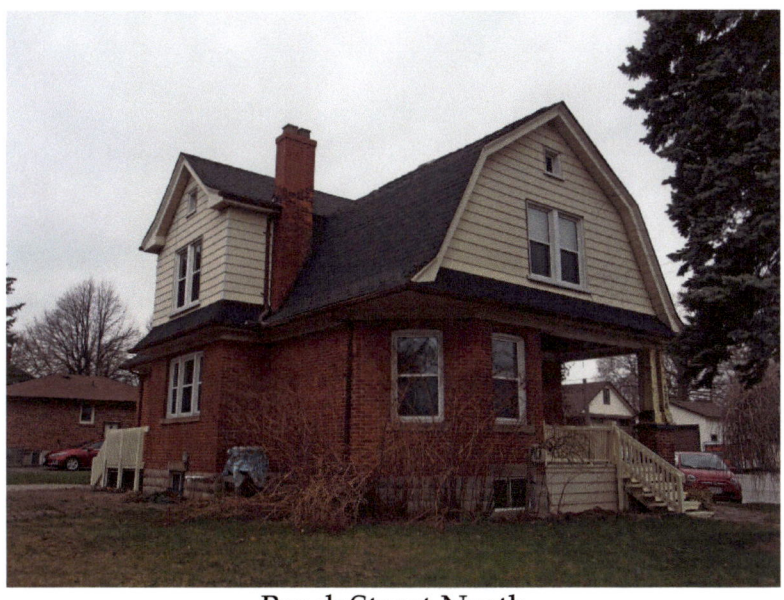
Brock Street North

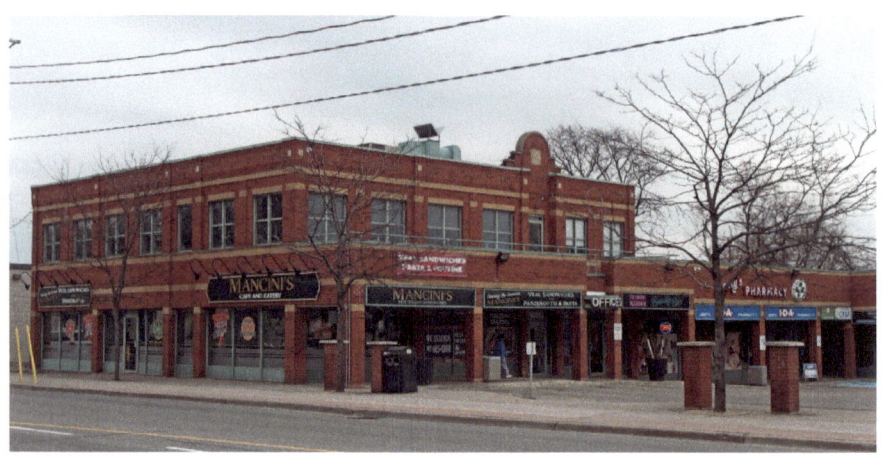
223 Brock Street North – Mancini's and Whitby Square

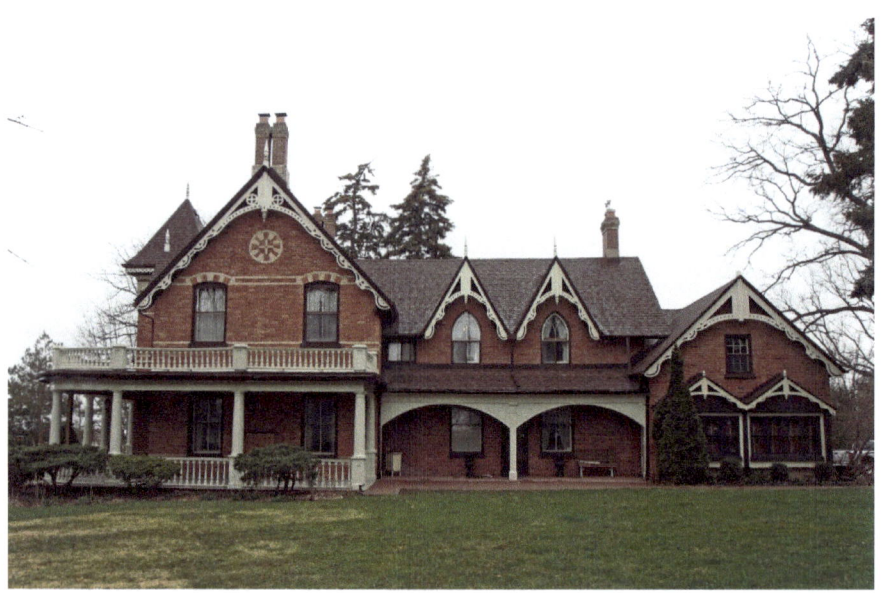
3050 Brock Street North – 1875 – Lakeview Hall

Building Styles

Arts and Crafts: The overlying theme - the house was based on the function of the house. Rooms were oriented to take advantage of the movement of the sun for warmth and light during daylight hours. Side entrances allowed for useable space on the front facade for light or garden use. Features include: wood, stone or stucco siding; low-pitched roof; wide eaves with triangular brackets; exposed roof rafters; porch with thick square or round columns; stone porch supports; exterior chimney made with stone; open floor plans with few hallways; many windows, some with stained or leaded glass; beamed ceilings; dark wood wainscoting and moldings; built-in cabinets, shelves, and seating.

Georgian, before 1860 – This style began with the British King Georges in the 18th century. These buildings have balanced facades around a central door, medium-pitched gable roofs, and small paned windows.

Gothic Revival, 1830-1890 – These decorative buildings have sharply-pitched gables with highly detailed verge boards, pointed-arch window openings, and dichromatic brickwork. It is a common style in Ontario.

Greek Revival – have gabled or hipped roofs with low pitches. The cornice of the main roof usually has a wide band which represents the entablature of classical Greek architecture consisting of the frieze and the architrave. Greek or Roman columns usually support the porch. The front door is surrounded by sidelights and a rectangular transom and is usually dressed with pilasters, pediments and/or columns.

Italianate, 1850-1900 – A two story rectangular building with a mild hip roof, a projecting frontispiece, and generous eaves with ornate cornice brackets was the basis of the style; often there are large sash windows, quoins, ornate detailing on the windows, belvederes and wraparound verandahs. Italianate commercial buildings often have cast iron cresting and elegant window surrounds.

Medieval Castle Architecture (from the Norman Invasion of 1066 to the Tudor dynasty of the Renaissance which ended in 1603) - The Architecture of Medieval castles were ambitious, state of the art castles of the Middle Ages. Medieval architecture ranged from the Romanesque Architecture style of the Normans, the Motte and Bailey design castles to the massive Norman Stone Castles with their towering stone keeps. The Romanesque style of Medieval Architecture moved on to the Edwardian Concentric castles used by the Plantagenet English King Edward I and then the slenderer and pointed style of the Gothic Medieval Architecture.

Neo-Classical, 1810-1850 – This style was a direct result of the War of 1812. Many Upper Canadians returning from the war with the United States were second or third generation Loyalists who had inherited land and means from their forefathers. Once the conflict had passed, they had the money and the time to expand their holdings and indulge their architectural whims. Both residential and commercial buildings were constructed on the traditional Georgian plan, but they had a new gaiety and light-heartedness. Detailing became more refined, delicate, and elegant.

Neo-Colonial (also Colonial Revival, Georgian Revival or Neo-Georgian) architecture seeks to revive elements of architectural style of American colonial architecture of the period around the Revolutionary War which drew strongly from Georgian architecture of Great Britain. Architecture from the 18th and early 19th centuries in Ontario includes a wide assortment of detailing and ornament applied to a design centered around the fireplace and the source of water. Structures are typically two stories, have a symmetrical front facade with elaborate front doorways, often with decorative crown pediments, fanlights, and sidelights, symmetrical windows flanking the front entrance, often in pairs or threes, and columned porches.

Prairie style, 1900-1940 - is one of the only purely North American styles. The horizontal lines, projecting eaves and geometric patterning of finishes and windows contrast sharply with the more formal, Classical styles taken from ancient Greece. Vernacular materials, stone, brick, and natural wood were preferred for finishes and often stained glass with patterns taken from nature was added. Prairie buildings are generally domestic and have a geometric patterning that is immediately evident. The complete lack of historicizing detail is deliberate and points to the trends found later in the century.

Queen Anne, 1885-1900 – This style is distinguished by an irregular outline featuring a combination of an offset tower, broad gables, projecting two-story bays, verandahs, multi-sloped roofs, and tall, decorative chimneys. A mixture of brick and wood is common. Windows often have one large single-paned bottom sash and small panes in the upper sash.

Regency Cottage, 1830-1860 – This style originated in England in 1815 and spread to Ontario later in the 19th century as British officers retired to Canada. It is a modest one-story house with a low-pitched hip roof and has a symmetrical front façade.

Renaissance Revival, 1870-1910 - The Renaissance Palazzo was a three- or four-story building with a rusticated (very large masonry blocks with deep joints and decorated with rough or bold finishes) ground floor, and regularized understated windows on two upper levels, always finished by an elaborate cornice. The Renaissance saw the development of a graceful and balanced adaptation of the Greek styles. In Ontario, the Renaissance was revived in commercial buildings, banks, offices, and churches in many towns. Most of the Renaissance Revival buildings are designed without columns while those with columns and pilasters are more ornate.

Second Empire, 1860-1880 – The mansard roof is the most noteworthy feature of this style and is evidence of the French origins. Projecting central towers and one or two-story bays can also be present.

Vernacular/Traditional Mode 1638 - 1950
Influenced but not defined by a particular style, vernacular buildings are made from easily available materials and exhibit local design characteristics.

Victorian - In Ontario, a Victorian style building can be seen as any building built between 1840 and 1900 that doesn't fit into any of the other categories. It encompasses a large group of buildings constructed in brick, stone, and timber, using an eclectic mixture of Classical and Gothic motifs.

Other Books by Barbara Raue

Coins of Gold
Arrows, Indians and Love
The Life and Times of Barbara
The Cromwell Family Book
Laura Secord Discovered
Daddy Where Are You?

Montana Series
Book 1: Montana Dream
Book 2: Life on the Montana Frontier
Book 3: Montana to Boston and Back
Book 4: Montana Sons Go to War
Book 5: Montana Sons Return from War

Donaldson Series
Book 1: Rite of Passage
Book 2: Rite of Marriage

© 2022 by Barbara Raue - All the photos in this book have been taken with my cameras. I own the rights to them.

Barbara is The Authority on Saving Our History One Photo at a Time. She is pursuing her interest in photography and architecture by preserving a record through photos of old buildings from the 1800s and 1900s with their unique architecture. Enjoy the beautiful architecture in the comfort of your living room. Dream about what it was like in those by-gone days. Dream about what it was like to live in a mansion like one of those in this book.

Barbara Raue, a wife, mother and grandmother, is an avid reader and writer. She has researched and compiled several family histories. In 2010, Barbara published her book "Coins of Gold," which celebrates the courageous life of her mother, May Todd. Barbara's second book is a historical fiction "Arrows, Indians and Love" which takes place in Boonesborough, Kentucky during the time of Daniel Boone. In 2013, Barbara published *The Cromwell Family Book* in which she traces her ancestry generations back into Great Britain. Her second novel is called *Laura Secord Discovered,* in which the story of Laura's service during the War of 1812 is shared. Barbara's memoir is titled *Daddy Where Are You?* It tells of her life growing up without a father. Five novels in the Montana Series have been published, *Montana Dream, Life on the Montana Frontier*, *Montana to Boston and Back, Montana Sons Go to War*, and *Montana Sons Return from War*. The Donaldson series of two novels is available: *Rite of Passage* and *Rite of Marriage.*

This is a link to Barbara's website to view all of her books
http://barbararaue.ca

www.ingramcontent.com/pod-product-compliance
Lightning Source LLC
Chambersburg PA
CBHW041941240526
45473CB00033B/151